Biblical

Resilience

By David Dickinson

Table of Contents

A Personal Story of Resilience

By Pastor Dave Dickinson

Dealing with a crisis, a major life change or major setback is an inescapable aspect of life. Whether it is a health crisis, a financial setback, loss of a job or a broken relationship there comes a time when each of us must face the necessity of bouncing back from the unimaginable. Resilience is defined as the "the capacity to recover quickly from difficulties." Resilience is the difference between the person whose response to a disaster incapacitates them leaving them unable to cope with life and another individual in the same situation who responds with a determination to come back and rise above the obstacles.

How we cope with adversity and react to a crisis demonstrates our ability to be resilient and recover from adversity and be ready to take on the challenges of life. Studies have shown that resilient people share a number of skills and abilities that keep them from being overwhelmed and overcome by their difficulties. In this book, we will explore some of the important characteristics of resilience which can, in fact, be developed and make one more capable of moving beyond the difficulties of life. As you proceed through the following pages, I want you to know that these truths have been lived and applied in real life and I am a testimony that these principles do in fact work.

A Victim of Tragedy

My own story of resilience began on November 28th, 1959, when I was only six years old. My family lived in Chicago and my father worked at the Santa Fe railroad while also studying at Northern Baptist Seminary to be a pastor. My father worked the overnight shift and one morning as we awoke for breakfast, I could read a real concern from my mother. Dad was usually home by this time, but today he wasn't. As the day went on the concern grew greater until finally, the police came to the door. My father was a "missing person." In the ensuing days, the concern and the questions just grew deeper. My dad's picture appeared on the front page of the Chicago papers and numerous church families and friends began dropping in. To a six-year-old, the only question that mattered was the one no one could answer, "Where's my daddy?"

As the days stretched into weeks, the visits from friends and police officers with questions slowed. There were no more news stories and the concerns became "What do we do now?" My mother had been a stay at home mother and I had three younger siblings. With four children, six and under, she had no choice but to go on welfare. We soon moved to a cheaper basement apartment in the Humboldt Park neighborhood. Life had changed dramatically!

The apartment had cracked and peeling paint and plaster. The neighborhood was definitely more dangerous. The one good thing about our new home was that we were just one block from our new church, Salem Evangelical Free Church. It was at Salem over the ensuing years, that I would find strength and support from people who genuinely loved our family and reached out to help.

The years that followed brought many new challenges. My brothers and sister had very limited memories of dad and my own memories were quickly fading. My mother was consumed with providing for four children on welfare and food stamps. My brother and I took on several paper routes when we were in elementary school, although, we were eventually forced to give them up due to the danger of being robbed frequently while collecting from customers.

I often wondered how life would have been different if my dad hadn't disappeared on that fateful day. I yearned for someone to teach me to play baseball and God brought a crippled boy named Mike into my life who had an endless knowledge of baseball despite the braces on his legs. I desired men I could look up to and God provided several Awana leaders through our church who sought to include me in their activities. I discovered quickly that I needed to be strong for my mother and younger siblings. I was the "man of the house."

During this time, my spiritual life was a source of strength. My mother frequently read the Bible with us had us in church every time there was an activity we could attend. But this was more than religion; this was a relationship with God that provided hope in the midst of discouraging circumstances. One Bible verse that was especially important during this time was John 1:12 "But as many as received him, to them gave he power to become the sons of God, even to them that believe on his name." While my earthly father was gone, I had a Heavenly Father who wanted me to be a part of His family, and He would never leave me.

A New Start

After seven long years in the inner city, 17 robbery attempts (including the same bicycle three times), and growing to be a teenager on the verge of starting high school, my mother went to court to have my father declared legally dead. This legal action would allow us to receive Social Security and Veteran's survivor's benefits and enable us to move out of the city of Chicago. After another year, due to an insurance company's fight to avoid paying a small life insurance policy, my father was declared legally dead. In my mind, I had long ago come to that conclusion. Somehow, my father must be dead. It was the only explanation that accounted for his being gone so long.

We immediately moved to western Nebraska to serve as winter caretakers of the Maranatha Bible Camp at Maxwell, Nebraska. Maxwell had a population at the time of 320, a far cry from the city of Chicago. To say this experience was culture shock is a gross understatement. There was the beauty of the camp and the great opportunities to learn and grow in the ministry of the camp. But there was also the feeling of being alone among a class of students who had been together since kindergarten, the alienation of living in a culture I didn't understand or really fit into.

As I had done in Chicago, I soaked up information, sought out mentors and tried new things I wasn't sure I could accomplish. Although I had started woefully behind my class academically, I finally managed to get on the honor roll as a senior. Although I was very small, I played football, basketball and ran the mile in track, none with much success, but all a new experience and an opportunity to discover myself and my abilities.

After four years of high school, I returned to Chicago to attend Moody Bible Institute and prepare for the pastoral ministry. After graduating from Moody, I met and married my wife and once again confronted the impact of not having a father. I didn't know how to be a husband or father, and many of the models around me were deeply flawed. Once again, I turned to my Bible and the advice of godly men I could trust as I stumbled and searched for how to lead a family.

The Case Reopened

As I began to raise my own family, I thought the final chapter of the story of my father had been written. The full story, however, was just beginning.

One afternoon, I received a phone call from my mother. She had been contacted by a representative of the Social Security

Administration. She explained that my father had been living under another identity for over 35 years and had been exposed only when he attempted to collect Social Security benefits under his assumed name.

Over the coming months, I would learn that my father intentionally chose to disappear that day in Chicago, created a new identity complete with a new Social Security number, met another woman and married her, and had three children, the oldest of whom is also named David. In the years since he disappeared, he had held jobs for which he was overqualified, so he wouldn't risk someone checking out his college education or background. He even used his theological education as he rose to leadership within his church.

A New Battle

The emotions that accompanied this revelation were overwhelming. I felt betrayed, abandoned and rejected amidst many other confusing feelings. As the days passed these feelings developed into deep feelings of anger and resentment about what my father had done to me.

Every aspect of my life was soon impacted by this revelation. I was distracted at my job, my work as a volunteer youth minister was suffering and I was becoming more distant with my wife and children. I discovered that anger was a poison working from within, eating away at me with every passing day.

A few months after the revelation, I led a youth trip of approximately 60 teenagers to a youth conference conducted by Dawson McAllister. His theme for the two-day conference was family conflict. In one session he discussed how to deal with hurts and anger over past wrongs. He talked about how anger repeatedly victimizes us even after the original hurt. He also warned that this anger usually results in our anger hurting those closest to us.

My wife and my three daughters were all in the audience that day, and I knew that I could not hold on to my anger at the risk of hurting them. I had to do what I did not want to do, forgive my father. I left the auditorium, sat down on the floor in a hallway and tearfully made the decision to let go of my anger toward my father. There were initially no feelings of forgiveness or compassion. It was simply a choice to release the anger building up inside of me. Making this choice didn't bring immediate results either. Over the next days and weeks, I found myself repeatedly affirming my decision to release my anger and choose not to dwell on what my dad had done. Gradually, those around me began to see the change and more importantly, I began to see the change in myself.

There were still some tough times, such as the first Thanksgiving, which had always marked the time that my father had disappeared. The memories and feelings would come rushing back and just as I was sinking into self-pity and bitterness, I would be reminded of my decision to forgive. My only recourse in those times was to ask God to give me the strength to once again walk away from the anger. Gradually, those episodes have become less frequent, and anger has been replaced with pity for a man who lived in hiding and missed a great relationship with me, my mother, brothers, and sister.

The years have passed, and my father and his second wife have both passed away. Although I did write to my father, I never had a relationship with my dad again. I have met and become good friends with my half brothers and sister. My own children are grown and have families of their own. I am so grateful that God caught me as I was slipping into anger and bitterness and that he provided for me the means of being resilient even in my darkest moments.

There have also been other challenges and times when I have had to go back again to these important principles and the timeless truths of God's Word, the Bible. These principles have brought me through financial setbacks and health challenges, the experience of raising three daughters and the counseling of others in times of crisis over more than 40 years of ministry.

The contents of this book on resilience are really a documentation of my own journey. Our lives never have to be defined by our past. The future is what we choose to make it today. My prayer for you is that you will join me on this exciting, life changing journey of resilience.

What is Biblical Resilience?

And Why is it Important Enough to Write a Book?

As a Pastor for the last forty years, I have applied the truth of Scripture to many areas of life. This has happened not only in my ministry but also in my personal life. I have found that Scripture speaks to virtually every area of our lives with direction that provides for Godly responses to our needs. One area of particular interest to me has long been that of resilience. *Resilience is the ability to have a constructive and productive response to a crisis or setback.*

Life will inevitably bring a variety of crisis situations. We may experience a financial crisis, a health crisis, a moral crisis, a relationship crisis, a spiritual crisis, or a career crisis. We cannot avoid crises in life. Therefore, resilience must begin with acknowledging that bad circumstances and hurt are not unexpected. Some people respond to a crisis with anger or shock, thinking, this should not have happened to them. This is unrealistic thinking. Not only do bad things sometimes happen to good people, but bad things happen to all people. You will not be an exception to the rule.

I am not saying that we should constantly be expecting the worst (that would be unrealistic pessimism), but that we should not be surprised when we encounter difficulties in life. So, if trials are a part of life for all of us, what is the purpose of trials? Difficulties and trials can serve several very important purposes in God's plan for our life.

The Bible frequently speaks of trials producing greater character and godliness in us. There are simply some lessons than can only be learned through times of difficulty and struggle.

But we also glory in our sufferings, because we know that suffering produces perseverance; perseverance, character; and character, hope. And hope does not put us to shame, because God's love has been poured out into our hearts through the Holy Spirit, who has been given to us.

Romans 5:3-5

Not only do trials produce character in us but trials in our lives are also used by God to bring us back into obedience to Him and His will. This is not just God being mean to get His way. His will for us is always what is also best for us. But when we stray from Him, he will often use trials and difficult times to draw us back to Him. Listen to what King David says in the Psalms about his experience while he tried to hide his adultery and murder:

When I kept silent, my bones wasted away through my groaning all day long. For day and night your hand was heavy on me; my strength was sapped as in the heat of summer. Then I acknowledged my sin to you and did not cover up my iniquity. I said, "I will confess my transgressions to the LORD." And you forgave the guilt of my sin.

Psalm 32:3-5

We have all experienced the kind of agony David describes when we are living in disobedience to God. God's conviction and the accompanying discomfort are designed to lead us to confession and forgiveness.

We must also recognize that there are times when trials neither teach us or discipline us, but are not related to our actions at all. We live in a sinful, fallen world and many things from natural disasters to criminal acts against innocent victims, cause us to question. Consider this exchange between Jesus and His disciples in the Gospel of John:

As he went along, he saw a man blind from birth. His disciples asked him, "Rabbi, who sinned, this man or his parents, that he was born blind?" "Neither this man nor his parents sinned," said Jesus, "but this happened so that the works of God might be displayed in him.

John 9:1-3

The disciples, apparently, believed that either this man or his parents were responsible for the trial he was now experiencing. Jesus makes clear that neither is responsible. In this case, God's plan was that Jesus' power would be validated through the healing of this man and that God would be glorified as a result.

The reality is that there are many times in life that the answer to our question, "Why am I suffering?" will go unanswered. It is still, however, critical that we find ways to move on with life. In the words of the song from Casting Crowns:

> "We know we were made for so much more
> Than ordinary lives
> It's time for us to more than just survive
> We were made to thrive"[1]

Resilience in these times of crisis is evidenced in three basic ways. Resilience helps to minimize the damage of minor hurts, it helps us recover from the larger blows in our life, and it helps us to prepare for future crises by learning from our present situation. Let's look at each of these in greater detail.

Resilience minimizes the damage of minor hurts.

We have all experienced, in our youth, those minor hurts that, at the time, seemed to be an insurmountable catastrophe. The loss of a first love (or infatuation), the embarrassment before your

---

[1] John Mark Hall / Matthew West "Thrive" lyrics © Sony/ATV Music Publishing LLC

peers, or the seemingly spectacular failure seemed much larger at the time than it really was. While these are normal experiences as teens, as we mature, we must become better able to minimize the damage from these kinds of experiences.

Resilience enables us to absorb minor shocks without being significantly hurt or damaged. This is more than just toughness. Toughness insulates us from feelings we need to function in relationships. Resilience is the strength to overlook a slight or minor hurt and not be wounded by insignificant issues. Sadly, it has become very acceptable to be easily offended and hurt by the slightest offense. Scripture, however, points to the importance of this valuable facet of wisdom in life.

> *A person's wisdom yields patience; it is to one's glory to overlook an offense.*

> Proverbs 19:11

Often something we take offense with is not intended as offensive or is a matter of a misunderstanding. It is important in these circumstances to consider the value of the relationship and be willing to discuss the problem or overlook the unintentional offense.

There are times that we should not overlook an offense. This is the case when the action is potentially harmful the person or to others or when the action could be part of a destructive pattern of behavior. We never want people to be hurt by our decision to overlook an offense. The bottom line is that love is to govern our decision to both deal with a hurtful situation or overlook an unintentional misunderstanding.

> *Above all, love each other deeply, because love covers over a multitude of sins.*

> 1 Peter 4:8

When we love someone, as God repeatedly commands in Scripture, we will be more willing to give some latitude in what offends us because the relationship with that person is more important to us than our minor hurts or offenses.

In a later chapter, we will look at distorted thinking that keeps us from seeing things realistically. It is critical that we not over-estimate or minimize these minor hurts, making it more difficult to deal with greater crises we are sure to face in the future.

Resilience helps us recover from a crisis

We have all seen people who faced a seemingly unsurmountable situation and, after being briefly knocked down, came back stronger than ever. We have also seen those who, unfortunately, crumbled under the pressure and never seemed to recover. I have often used the example of an egg and a ping-pong ball. Both are similar in appearance, but when dropped on the floor, they experience drastically different results. While the ping-pong ball bounces back, the egg is irreparably damaged. It becomes useless for its original purpose (admittedly that purpose is not bouncing on the floor). We all want to be more like the ping-pong ball and less like the egg.

Resilience helps us to bounce back from those situations that may hurt us and knock us down. One thing is certain. You will encounter serious obstacles in life that will knock you down. The temptation at that moment will be to give up, but that cannot be an option. We must find ways, no matter how devastating the blow, to get back up, recover and move on with life.

The Bible is full of examples of people who overcame incredible obstacles and rebounded from seeming disasters in their lives to be used by God in amazing ways. Consider just a few examples:

- Abraham lied, claiming his wife was his sister to protect himself, even though he could have lost his wife.

- Moses killed a man in a fit of anger.

- David committed adultery and murder and thought he could get away with it.

- Jeremiah suffered from depression.

- Peter was impulsive and denied Jesus three times on the night Jesus needed him most.

- Paul persecuted and imprisoned Christians.

All of these men were ultimately used by God in mighty ways despite their weaknesses and failures. In fact, I believe that one of the reasons these historical characters are recorded in Scripture is so that we will see how real people have been able to respond to real trials and be victorious. One of my favorite Scriptures (and the theme verse for the church I pastor), is in Romans and speaks to the hope we find in these accounts:

> *For everything that was written in the past was written to teach us, so that through the endurance taught in the Scriptures and the encouragement they provide we might have hope.*

Romans 15:4

Resilience requires endurance in trials, and encouragement in those times we are tempted to give up, to be able to overcome the trying times we may experience. It is in Scripture and in our relationship with God that we find these resources.

Resilience helps us to prepare for future crises by learning from our present situation.

Resilience teaches us to look for lessons to be learned in every circumstance that will make us more resilient in the future. Mistakes are often costly, and it is in our best interest to learn from those mistakes the first time and not repeat the mistakes and the accompanying consequences.

Even better is learning from the mistakes of others. There are several great sources for these lessons. One way of learning from the mistakes of others is to watch and learn from friends or family. The problem is, we may not always recognize a mistake at that moment. An even better source is implied by the previous passage of Scripture. We can learn from the written record of Scripture and have the benefit of the Bible's analysis of each event and decision.

How do we develop resilience?

Is a person born with natural resilience or is resilience something we can learn and develop? While skills and intelligence may influence our ability to be resilient, there is ample evidence that many very skilled and intelligent people are not resilient. I believe that much of what is required to be resilient can be learned. Admittedly, if the opposite conclusion were true, there would be no point in writing this book. In the following pages, we will be developing some of the ways we can learn to become more resilient.

Learning life's lessons is critical to reducing the number and severity of the trials we bring on ourselves in the future. We can never completely eliminate trials because many trials are beyond our control, but, if we reduce those trials that we are responsible for creating, we can significantly improve our lives. This aspect of resilience works to eliminate the crisis before it begins and before it knocks us down.

We will begin our discussion with the "Enemies of Resilience." These characteristics will disrupt our ability to be resilient, either by distorting how we see our choices or by limiting our ability to bounce back in a time of crisis. Often these are emotional responses that hold us back from being successful. Dealing with these enemies of resilience prepares us to better deal with a future crisis.

The second section of this book looks at some of the underlying beliefs that build resilience. If we believe that resilience can be learned, we must consider, what are the things we need to learn to be resilient? Resilience requires wisdom in our decision making, supportive relationships, and the ability to effect change in our own lives. These chapters will take you through the beliefs that build greater resilience and put us in a better position to recover from traumatic events.

Questions for Thought and Discussion

1. How have you seen difficult times in your life make you stronger?

2. What are some examples of "minor hurts" that we can and should overlook without resulting in damage or further hurt?

3. How do you feel, understanding that many Bible characters overcame obstacles and deep personal flaws on their way to being used mightily by God?

4. What are some examples of encouragement we can find in Scripture? What passages have helped you to be resilient?

5. What are some important life lessons you have learned from failures or crises situations?

Enemies of Resilient Thinking

Distorted Thinking

Anger

Fear

Guilt and Shame

Pride

Habits and Addictions

Distorted Thinking

When we encounter a crisis in our lives, and it is most critical that we make the best possible decisions, our thinking is often clouded or distorted. This distortion is illustrated here by the image of the fun-house mirrors. While none of us would mistake these images for reality, we are often fooled by the

distorted patterns in how we view the world around us and events that impact our lives. This distorted thinking results in an inaccurate view of the situation and consequently leads to poor decisions and an even deeper crisis in the future. The first step to addressing a crisis is to get a clear picture of our situation so that we can make the best decisions about how to deal with the crisis.

> *There is a way that seems right to a man, but in the end it leads to death.*

> Proverbs 14:12

In this lesson, we will look at some common distortions in our thinking. These distortions have the impact of making it more difficult to overcome obstacles and setbacks in our life because we do not see the problems accurately.

Whenever significant events, especially negative events happen in our life, it is important that we see these events accurately to learn from them and overcome any lasting difficulties. There are two extremes that are both wrong and not very helpful in these circumstances. The first is to over-dramatize the significance of a situation, blowing everything out of proportion. The second and opposite response is to minimize the situation, refusing to accept that life changes may be necessary to avoid this kind of occurrence in the future.

The Distortion of Over-Dramatizing

Over-dramatizing is an emotional response that sees negative events or failures as being more dramatic or impactful than they really are. Feelings of embarrassment, disappointment and vulnerability are felt more intensely and seen as more significant than a more objective analysis would conclude. While it is impossible to be completely objective in the midst of pain, it is important to see events accurately to be able to move on. Some examples of this over-dramatization are:

- The teen experiencing their first romantic break-up with their first serious boyfriend or girlfriend. In the moment, this seems overwhelming, but most adults know that you can survive and move on with life. The pain is real and intense, but it is not the end of our life.

- A person who experiences a significant financial setback or even a bankruptcy and feels they will never recover. While there may be some real consequences, once again recovery and resilience are possible.

- The victim of bullying or public embarrassment feels that they will never overcome the embarrassment or fear of the bully. The reality is that we can take charge of our future, even in these circumstances and overcome the adversity.

Assumptions:

Over-dramatizing requires some assumptions that do not accurately reflect reality and therefore work to distort our perceptions of past or current circumstances.

- The first assumption is that we can or should depend on our emotions as an accurate response to our circumstances. Making this worse is the message of our culture that we should "follow our feelings." The reality is that feelings are often unreliable and overly intense.

- The second assumption is that the past experiences dictate our future and that past failures and hurts cannot be overcome. The point of this book is to counter this belief and show that there is nothing we cannot overcome with God's strength and the power of resilience.

Dangers:

There are many dangers to over-dramatizing a situation, but I would like to focus on two dangers that can make a significant difference.

- Over-dramatizing usually makes situations worse, not better. As the drama grows, so do the consequences of the action.

- Over-dramatizing also creates the illusion that problems are too big and cannot be resolved. This, then, can lead to depression and even thoughts or attempts at suicide.

The Truth:

If over-dramatization is a distortion, what is the truth? While past actions do carry significant consequences, they can be overcome and do not dictate our future. The reality is that in God's power, any problem can be overcome. History is full of people who overcame overwhelming obstacles to live resilient lives.

An Example from Scripture:

One example that stands out from the Bible is the life of Moses. Moses, although he was an Israelite, was miraculously spared by God and raised in the house of Pharaoh, the king of Egypt. One day, we are told, Moses saw an Egyptian abusing an Israelite, and he responded in anger, killing the Egyptian. The next day, he discovered that his secret was out, and he feared that surely the king would find out what he had done. In fear, Moses decided to flee to the desert where he lived in anonymity for the next 40 years.

God then revealed to Moses that He wanted Moses to go back to Egypt, the place of his failure, to lead the Israelites out of slavery in Egypt. Moses offers several hollow excuses to God before finally submitting to God's plan for him. Moses went on to be one of the greatest leaders in recorded history, bringing Israel out of slavery and establishing, what we still see as the foundation for moral law when he received the Ten Commandments from God.

The Distortion of Minimizing

While the distortion of over-dramatizing made a problem appear to be bigger than it really was, it is also possible to distort reality through minimizing. Minimizing attempts to downplay the significance of an event or its consequences resulting in failing to take events seriously that could drastically affect one's life. Some examples of minimization are:

- Teenagers or young adults often display an air of invincibility that minimizes the risks and consequences of their behavior. All too often, this results in life-altering or even deadly consequences.

- One perfect example of minimizing is the all too frequent response heard after an apology, "That's OK. It didn't hurt." The reality is often this is a mask for the very real hurt that was inflicted.

Assumptions:

Minimizing reality also requires certain erroneous assumptions. These assumptions work to either ignore or downplay real consequences.

- Minimizing almost always assumes, that while some people may experience negative consequences, we will not be among those unfortunate enough to be hurt. Often those who minimize, assume that their superior intellect, skills or luck will protect them from the damage others experience.

- Minimizing sometimes even denies the reality of the potential consequences. Denials of the addictive potential of certain drugs is a great example of this assumption.

- Minimizing also sometimes operates on the assumption that our present experience is all that really matters. Concern about the future is seen as restricting our freedom of experience in the present. To this person, no risk is too great if the thrill is great enough.

Dangers:

Several obvious dangers are evident when we minimize what could be very real and impactful consequences. Obviously, this person will probably experience more hurt and tragedy than the person who looks at situations with a more realistic view, but I would like to focus on other dangers that affect our ability to be resilient.

- The first danger is that we fail to acknowledge there is a problem even when it is evident to others. This results in

27

our not even attempting to solve the problem since, in our view, there is no problem.

- Minimizing risks and consequences will also have a negative effect on our judgment in solving our problems, once we admit there is a problem. A high-risk solution to a problem is seldom a very reliable choice.

The Truth:

The truth is that whether we minimize consequences or over-dramatize the consequences we face the result is that we are not making decisions based on reality. The best decisions are made when we see things as they really are, and we are making decisions based on facts, not on the way we want, or fear, things to be.

An Example from Scripture:

The younger son in Jesus' story of the Prodigal Son is a great example of this form of distorted thinking. He sought to get his inheritance early, so he could spend it living high in his youth. His decision to leave home and spend his fortune on immediate pleasures is an example of minimizing concern for the future and the consequences of present decisions. The result of his decisions left him penniless and, but for the compassion of his father, he would have faced a bleak future.

Either of these distortions results in our not solving our problems, either because we believe the problem is unsolvable or because we deny the existence of the problem. An approach based in reality views problems accurately and sees both the dangers and the solutions that will lead to our being resilient. Consider this passage and note the balance Paul has in viewing his problems accurately without minimizing or over-dramatizing.

But we have this treasure in jars of clay to show that this all-surpassing power is from God and not from us. We are hard pressed on every side, but not crushed; perplexed, but not in despair; persecuted, but not abandoned; struck down, but not destroyed...

Therefore we do not lose heart. Though outwardly we are wasting away, yet inwardly we are being renewed day by day. For our light and momentary troubles are achieving for us an eternal glory that far outweighs them all. So we fix our eyes not on what is seen, but on what is unseen. For what is seen is temporary, but what is unseen is eternal.

2 Corinthians 4:7-9, 16-18

In this passage, Paul begins with the reference to "treasures in jars of clay." This is an important reference that may not be immediately obvious. In biblical times, potters would set out to make a commissioned piece of pottery and would cast several vessels on their potter's wheel, with the assumption that while some would meet the standards of their customer, other pieces would ultimately be revealed to have flaws and imperfections making them nearly worthless. These flawed vessels would be labeled "jars of clay" and sold at a deeply discounted price. The point in the passage is that Christ living in us is the treasure, while we are flawed and imperfect.

Note that Paul's hope is based both on a real view of circumstances, but also on a confidence in God. His view of his situation is neither over-dramatized or minimized, but accurately perceived.

Ultimately, our hope is in the inner renewal of God, giving us strength for each day. While we cannot always see God's hand at work in our struggles, we can be confident in His power and care for us.

Principles for Resilient Thinking

Having examined some of the significant distortions people use in their approach to life, I feel it is important to look at some steps we can take to protect ourselves from distorted thinking. In this section, we will focus on several Scripture passages that guide us to more realistic and resilient thinking.

Don't always trust your own understanding

Trust in the LORD with all your heart and lean not on your own understanding; in all your ways acknowledge him, and he will make your paths straight. Do not be wise in your own eyes; fear the LORD and shun evil. This will bring health to your body and nourishment to your bones.

Proverbs 3:5-8

These verses from the opening chapters of the book of Proverbs in the Bible, repeatedly warn us to check out our own thinking and conclusions. We need to begin with the understanding that our judgments are often clouded by emotions, incomplete information, past experiences or pressures from others that will result in our making bad decisions unless we take a step back and look at the circumstances more objectively or with help that can speak truth to us.

Much of what we have looked at in this chapter can be seen in the light of thinking with our emotions. Emotional thinking often leads to poor decisions made when our emotions have overridden our better judgment and lead to great pain and regret later. Sometimes, it is important to delay a decision until we are less emotional or able to consult with a more objective source of counsel.

We also need to recognize distortions to which we are most vulnerable and make considerations for that area of weakness.

For example, if you know that you tend to dramatize situations you might want to seek out those friends who can help you with a dose of reality when you begin to spiral out of control. Having people in our life who can be objective and realistic while having the courage to speak the truth to us in the moment, is of incredible value.

Ultimately, however, the best source for tempering our distorted thinking, according to this passage, is to consult God. Trusting God and His Word, the Bible will always protect us from a distorted view of reality.

How do we do this? We must begin with a knowledge of Scripture that will require us to be reading and reflecting daily on His Word. As we do this, we need to consistently check our conclusions against the truth of Scripture. This will require that we be regularly reading and studying the Bible to be familiar with its teaching.

Don't conform your thinking to the world around you

Do not conform any longer to the pattern of this world, but be transformed by the renewing of your mind. Then you will be able to test and approve what God's will is—his good, pleasing and perfect will.

Romans 12:2

See to it that no one takes you captive through hollow and deceptive philosophy, which depends on human tradition and the basic principles of this world rather than on Christ.

Colossians 2:8

These two passages both draw attention to the second problem facing one who desires to think realistically. The culture we live in (and this has been true for all of recorded time) is in opposition to Biblical principles. We cannot allow the principles of the world around us to shape our thinking and expect to make the kind of decisions that are consistent with the truth of God's Word. Instead, we must consciously transform our thinking to be consistent with God's will. It is only then that we will know the best that God has for us.

Focus your mind on healthy thoughts

Finally, brothers, whatever is true, whatever is noble, whatever is right, whatever is pure, whatever is lovely, whatever is admirable—if anything is excellent or praiseworthy—think about such things. Whatever you have learned or received or heard from me, or seen in me—put it into practice. And the God of peace will be with you.

Philippians 4:8-9

Taking control of our thoughts is essential if we want to avoid distorted thinking. One means of doing this is to focus on thinking that is consistent with Godly purposes. This differs from just positive or optimistic thinking, in that it constantly asks, "How can my thinking be aligned with God and His plans?" As Paul says above, this thinking results in peace. And as verse 13 says, later in the chapter, this gives complete confidence since God gives us the strength.

I can do everything through him who gives me strength.

Philippians 4:13

Trust in God leads to a steadfast mind

You will keep in perfect peace him whose mind is steadfast, because he trusts in you. Trust in the LORD forever, for the LORD, the LORD, is the Rock eternal.

Isaiah 26:3-4

When we put our trust in God, our thinking is transformed from being distorted by emotions, distortions in our perceptions or the influence of the culture to what Isaiah describes as a "steadfast mind" that is at peace. This mind is at peace because it sees life accurately and responds with decisions that are informed by the truth of God's Word and rests in His promises and protection.

Questions for Thought and Discussion

1. Are you more likely to over-dramatize your problems or minimize your problems?

2. In what ways has distorted thinking about your problems or challenges kept you from being more resilient?

3. Why do we have to sometimes check the accuracy of our own thinking?

4. How are we influenced to think like the world around us and what are some ways we can counter this effect?

5. How are you most vulnerable to distorted thinking?

Enemies of Resilience

Anger

Before reading this chapter, I would encourage you to read my personal story of resilience at the front of this book, if you haven't already. This enemy of resilience has been intensely personal in my own life, and the lessons shared here are the result of personally struggling in this area.

Anger has devastating effects on many areas of our lives. Physically, our health cannot withstand prolonged anger, rage and resentment. Anger disrupts our ability to do our jobs, work well with others and get ahead in life. Most importantly, anger results in long-term damage to relationships within families and among friends.

When we encounter a major crisis in life, many times, we find anger at the foundation of the crisis. Even if anger has not been the cause of the crisis, it can be the reason we find it difficult to overcome the obstacles we face. In this lesson, we will look at three aspects of anger and some important Biblical principles for dealing with anger in ways that will enable us to be resilient in every area of our lives.

As we look at these three types of anger, we will be comparing them to universal warning symbols used to indicate the presence of various hazardous materials. This is appropriate since anger can be extremely hazardous to our resilience. Anger blinds us to good decisions and can be crippling in overcoming a crisis. To be resilient, we must learn to recognize the hazard of anger and take the important steps to protect ourselves from its damage.

Explosive Anger – Violent Rage

Anger that erupts into verbal or physical violence is explosive anger. Most often, the expression of this anger is way out of proportion to the action that triggered the anger. Examples of this anger are a loss of temper, physical violence, and destruction  of property. As I was growing up, I struggled with this type of anger. I was told that because I had red hair, I surely had a hot temper (I am not sure, yet, what that has to do with anger). Initially, I saw this as a license to lose my temper, but as I began to grow in my faith, I began to see that God never granted a "red hair" exception to His instructions concerning anger. The reality is that violent temper is sin and is damaging.

Many lives have been damaged by violent rage. This includes not only the victims or targets of the anger but also the one displaying the violent temper. This form of anger leads to violent assaults and property damage that is not only destructive to relationships but can also be criminal.

Controlling Violent Rage

In facing the problem of violent anger, we must begin with the understanding that this is damaging, and we must eliminate it from our lives. We need to determine to get explosive anger under control – no more excuses. As the following passage states, "get rid" of the anger.

> Get rid of all bitterness, rage and anger, brawling and slander, along with every form of malice.

> Ephesians 4:31

We must also recognize the seriousness of angry outbursts. Your anger interferes with all of your relationships, even your relationship with God. Jesus, referring to the Ten Commandments equated anger with murder. Some might want to challenge this since murder has such serious consequences, but Jesus recognized that the root of murder is often anger, which once it is unleashed is difficult to harness.

> "You have heard that it was said to the people long ago, 'Do not murder, and anyone who murders will be subject to judgment.'
> But I tell you that anyone who is angry with his brother will be subject to judgment...
> "Therefore, if you are offering your gift at the altar and there remember that your brother has something against you, leave your gift there in front of the altar. First go and be reconciled to your brother; then come and offer your gift.

Matthew 5:21-24

In the last verse of this passage, we are told that even if we have come to worship, it is important to deal with our anger first. We must always deal with anger immediately. Suppressed anger only gets worse. Talk it out and resolve disagreements while they are small. Take a short time-out if necessary to cool off, but commit to resolving the issue as soon as possible. Paul also, instructs us to deal with anger immediately so that we do not give the devil an opportunity to do greater damage in our lives.

> "In your anger do not sin": Do not let the sun go down while you are still angry and do not give the devil a foothold.

Ephesians 4:26-27

Quickly resolving our anger, recognizing its devastating potential is critical to avoiding the destructiveness of "Explosive Anger."

Flammable Anger – Verbal Anger

Flammable anger often starts much more slowly and quietly than explosive anger, but its consequences can be just as damaging. This form of anger seeks to inflict hurt on the object of our anger by the things we say. Examples of verbal anger are insults, name calling, gossip, and lies.

While the old saying is that "Sticks and stones will break my bones, but words will never hurt me," it simply isn't true. Words can inflict hurt that lasts a lifetime, and once something is said it can spread like wildfire and can never be retracted.

In our comparison, we are comparing this form of anger to an out-of-control fire. A few years ago, there were reports of a forest employee who wanted to be seen as a hero, so he started a small fire with the intention of letting it burn for a while and then being a hero by putting it out. His plan spun out of control when he was unable to put the fire out. The fire went on to burn out of control destroying vast areas of forest and creating significant property damage.

Quenching Verbal Anger

The things we say can be as destructive as violent actions. Don't minimize the damage this anger can inflict on others. All too often, we excuse the things we say with statements like, "I was just being honest" or "That's just how I am." The truth is that we are doing great damage to the people around us with the words that we say. This is especially true for impressionable children. James describes the things we say in this way:

The tongue also is a fire, a world of evil among the parts of the body. It corrupts the whole person, sets the whole course of his life on fire, and is itself set on fire by hell.

James 3:16

We should never minimize the impact of words spoken in anger. The effects of what we say can be felt for years and can change the course of a life. I frequently counsel with people who have been hurt by the words of a parent or others they looked up to, and are still impacted years later.

We must watch everything that comes out of our mouth. It's always better to think before we speak. Like your mother said, "If you can't say something good, don't say anything at all."

Do not let any unwholesome talk come out of your mouths, but only what is helpful for building others up according to their needs, that it may benefit those who listen.

Ephesians 4:29

The standard of only speaking that which builds others up may sound difficult to maintain, but how much better it is than to hurt people we care about with carelessly spoken words of anger. The secret to controlling what comes out of our mouth is to first clean up what resides in our heart. What comes out of your mouth started in your mind and heart. Don't allow yourself to even think angry thoughts or vengeful plans.

The good man brings good things out of the good stored up in his heart, and the evil man brings evil things out of the evil stored up in his heart. For out of the overflow of his heart his mouth speaks.

Luke 6:45

The apostle Paul instructs us to let everything we say reflect both truth and love. Truth without love can be mean, and love without

38

truth is deceptive. Together truth and love can build up those around us and keep us from the devastating effects of flammable anger.

> *Instead, speaking the truth in love, we will in all things grow up into him who is the Head, that is, Christ.*

Ephesians 4:15

Corrosive Anger – Bitterness, Unresolved Anger

Corrosive anger is not as visible as the previous two kinds of anger, but may even be the most damaging to the person consumed by this form of anger. Bitterness is anger that is unresolved and often suppressed or even denied. Examples of unresolved anger are unresolved conflicts, past abuse and hurt feelings.

This form of anger can last for years after the initial hurt and can have a devastating impact on a person. "Silent suffering" often results in physical problems such as ulcers and high blood presser, strained relationships and the inability to enjoy life. Even worse is that this form of anger eventually results in our lashing out at others who may not have even been involved in the initial hurt and damaging the lives of those we love.

As I personally dealt with this form of anger in my relationship with my father, I discovered what I have called the cycle of victimization. It is a predictable cycle that begins when we are victimized by someone else. We are the victim, and someone else has victimized us.

The next step in the cycle involves our anger toward the person who has victimized us. At this stage, the person who hurt us may not even know or care that we are angry, but the anger begins to have devastating effects as it eats away at us from the inside. Interestingly, at this point, we have become both the victim (the one being hurt) and the victimizer (the one inflicting the hurt).

Once we have been consumed for a period of time by our anger, the anger begins to seek an outlet. Unfortunately, it is most likely that those who will become the victim of our anger are those closest to us. In this stage of the cycle, we are still suffering from the hurts we have suffered, but we are also continuing the victimization by hurting someone else out of our anger.

The Cycle of Victimization		
Action	*Victim*	*Victimizer*
The Hurt	You	Others
The Anger	You	You
The Rage	Others	You

The key to stopping this cycle is to stop the unresolved anger before it consumes us and victimizes others.

Resolving Bitterness

The big question is how do we resolve this anger in a way that will not lead to ourselves and others being hurt? The only solution for bitterness is forgiveness, forgiveness modeled by Jesus Christ.

> *Get rid of all bitterness, rage and anger, brawling and slander, along with every form of malice. Be kind and compassionate to one another, forgiving each other, just as in Christ God forgave you.*

> Ephesians 4:31-32

Our first reaction to this suggestion may be to reject any idea of extending forgiveness to someone who has hurt us badly. I often hear things like "I can never forgive that person." I believe our rejection of this path to healing is most often rooted in a complete misunderstanding of the Biblical concept of forgiveness.

Understanding Forgiveness

The first thing we need to know is that forgiveness is not a feeling, it is a choice to no longer hang on to the anger. Turning a feeling on and off is, at best, a difficult prospect, but choosing to not hold on to the anger (which is also hurting us) is something we can accomplish. You do not have to "feel" like forgiving to forgive someone.

Forgiveness is also not something we do for the benefit of the offender, but something we do as part of our own healing. If we hold on to the anger, we can never get past the hurt, but once we release the anger, we can begin to heal.

Forgiveness does not require that the offender be sorry or even ask for forgiveness. This could be a real barrier to our healing, since the person who hurt us may not care that they hurt us or may be out of our life or may even have died. If forgiveness required the offender to be sorry, then those whose offender was unable or unwilling to express sorrow would be forever trapped in their hurt. It is important that we not wait for the offender to be sorry because, frankly, that may never happen.

Forgiveness does not excuse the sin. This may be the biggest misconception concerning forgiveness. Many are reluctant to forgive because they mistakenly believe that this will excuse what was done. Nothing could be further from the truth! Forgiveness recognizes that the offense was evil and can only be dealt with by forgiveness. It acknowledges that there is nothing that either we or the one who hurt us can do to undo the evil and the hurt that has been done. The only way we can move forward with our life is to make the choice to release our anger through forgiveness. In the above verse from Ephesians, we are told to forgive as God forgave us. God did not excuse our sin. He chose to send His Son, Jesus, to pay the penalty for our sin and for the sins of the world. Our sins (and the sins of those who have hurt us) are forgiven by God only when we put our trust in Jesus Christ.

Forgiveness does not deny the hurt. We don't have to pretend that we weren't hurt or that we still don't hurt over what was done. It does require that we give up the right to be angry and with it the continued pain brought about by that anger.

Forgiveness does not remove the consequences. The consequences for the action may be unaffected. There may still be criminal penalties, severed relationships and certain protections that must remain in place. The real issue is that the anger has been dealt with.

Forgiveness does not always restore the relationship. The future relationship may still not be safe. Forgiveness does not require the victim to place themselves or their loved ones in danger by restoring the relationship as if nothing has happened. Something evil has happened and sometimes, even though we are no longer angry, the relationship may be unsafe or irretrievably broken.

How do we choose to forgive?

Forgiveness is a choice to not hold on to anger. Understanding this, there are three things we must commit to do:

First, we must commit to not dwell on the incident. The more time you spend thinking about the hurt and the injustice, the harder it will be to get past the anger and the longer it will take to heal.

Second, we must commit to not bring up the offense and use it against our offender. We cannot truly forgive while we are attempting to hurt our offender or seek revenge for what has been done. God tells us that seeking revenge is for Him alone.

Third, we must commit to not spread our anger to others by talking about the offender. The purpose of this is to not attempt to turn others against the offender. It does not preclude testifying in court, or sharing as part of therapy or bringing healing to yourself or others.

Forgiveness doesn't mean that our feelings are immediately changed. My own experience was that it took an extended time for my feelings to begin to change. In fact, I believe this may be part of the application in a discussion between Jesus and Peter in the Bible:

> *Then Peter came to Jesus and asked, "Lord, how many times shall I forgive my brother when he sins against me? Up to seven times?" Jesus answered, "I tell you, not seven times, but seventy times seven.*

Matthew 18:21-22

Forgiveness may need to be repeated over an extended period of time, but it is the only way we can truly experience healing and wholeness again.

Forgiveness releases you from the anger!

Questions for Thought and Discussion

1. Of the three types of anger discussed in this chapter, (explosive, flammable and corrosive) which would you be most likely to struggle with?

2. In what ways is murder equated with anger? Why is it important to quickly deal with explosive anger?

3. In what ways have you been hurt by angry words in the past? Has this led to your being more careful or less careful about the things you say to others in anger?

4. What are the biggest barriers to giving up bitterness and forgiving those who have hurt us?

5. What is or could be your motivation to forgive those who have hurt you?

Enemies of Resilience
Fear

The Role of Fear in Our Lives

Fear plays some very important roles in our lives as it helps us to assess risk in our lives. Fear of consequences may keep us from doing things that are dangerous or illegal. Fear of the future or the unknown may lead us to make certain preparations we would not otherwise consider.

But, fear can also be disabling and hold us back from taking the steps we need to be resilient in life. Fear can keep us from taking even reasonable risks that could help us recover from a crisis. Fear of embarrassment could keep us from taking steps to get help when we need it.

As we assess the role of fear in our lives, I would like to consider the role of fear in three distinct zones. Not everyone will have things placed in the same zone and, in fact, most people will find things moving from one zone to another over time. The three zones are depicted in this diagram:

- Events in our comfort zone elicit little fear. These are things we do almost automatically without ever considering risks or dangers.

- Events in our challenge zone are accompanied with a sense of caution that heightens our attention and focus. Over time, some of these events may move eventually to the comfort zone.

- Fear keeps us from attempting tasks in our danger zone and is a source of self-protection. The problem comes when we place things in the danger zone that we need to be able to accomplish in order to be successful and resilient.

Consider some examples of events you would place in each of these zones:

- ○ Your Comfort Zone -

- ○ Your Courage Zone -

- ○ Your Danger Zone -

The Focuses of Fear

Fear can be focused in a number of different directions and it is important to identify the focus of our fear in order to address it effectively. In each of the following, fear can function in a positive way to alert us to risks and dangers, but can also lead to a failure to have the courage necessary to live life to the fullest.

- Fear of consequences – As noted earlier, this can sometimes be helpful, but it is important to remember that sometimes the consequences of a right action are difficult and uncomfortable

- Fear of the uncontrollable – People and situations are often beyond our personal control and are not predictable. Personal relationships are among the least controllable situations (as any parent of teenagers can attest), but they are often the most rewarding as well.

- Fear of the unknown and the future – No one can truly know the future. Virtually everything we do comes with certain risks or a certain level of unpredictability. Each person needs to determine the amount of risk they are comfortable in taking.

- Fear of failure – Everything we attempt brings the potential for both success and failure. Fear focuses on the possibility of failure rather than the potential for success.

- Fear of death – This may be the greatest fear of all for most people, and yet it is a universal experience.

The Many Faces of Fear

Fear presents itself in many different ways. Some of the most common expressions of fear are:

- Anxiety and worry – This is one of the most common ways we respond to fear. We spend much time and energy thinking about the object of our fear and heighten our anxiety over the potential problem. The fact is that many, if not most, of the things we worry about never actually happen. Worry can be physically and emotionally damaging, taking a toll on our health and relationships.

- Withdrawal and avoidance – Some people choose to just avoid people or places that are associated with fear in their minds. They don't go to a place because it brings back fearful memories or they avoid people they feel are threatening. The problem with this is that our lives are soon governed by the growing list of places or people we find threatening and we withdraw from much of life.

- Acting out to divert attention – Sometimes a false sense of bravado or acting out is a sign of the fear of having to deal with a situation. The student would rather disrupt the class than have everyone know he doesn't understand what is being taught.

- Damaged relationships – Fear leads us to become defensive and create distance in some of our closest relationships. Anyone who is dominated by fear has difficulty reaching out and caring for others which naturally hampers good relationships.

- Escape into addictive behaviors – Fear often drives us to seek an escape from certain people, situations or feelings. Too often this escape is found either in addictive substances, such as drugs or alcohol, or in addictive behaviors, such as gambling or pornography.

Fear can be crippling when we cannot move beyond our comfort zone to accomplish necessary tasks or when we are held back by irrational fears. Fear also limits our relationships and makes us a captive of our own fears. A life lived in fear will result in an ever-smaller comfort zone and significant regrets over what might have been, if only we had the courage.

Dealing with Fear!

How do we overcome our fears, particularly those fears that hold us back from accomplishing all that God would have us to be and do. Paul provides us with a formuls for dealing with our fears in the following passage:

For God did not give us a spirit of timidity (fear), but a spirit of power, of love and of self-discipline.

2 Timothy 1:7

Power

Many of our fears center in our sense of powerlessness and the reality is that much of life is beyond our power to control. The reality is that in our own strength, many of our challenges are beyond our abilities. In our relationship with God, however, we draw on His limitless power to overcome our fears.

> *Do you not know? Have you not heard? The LORD is the everlasting God, the Creator of the ends of the earth. He will not grow tired or weary, and his understanding no one can fathom. He gives strength to the weary and increases the power of the weak. Even youths grow tired and weary, and young men stumble and fall; but those who hope in the LORD will renew their strength. They will soar on wings like eagles; they will run and not grow weary, they will walk and not be faint.*

Isaiah 40:28-31

The prophet Isaiah begins this passage with a description of God as Creator and everlasting God to emphasize the considerable power he wields, and then moves quickly to the application of that power. Because of His power and understanding, our weakness really doesn't matter. In fact, he promises to give strength to those who are tired, weak and stumbling. This is important in our discussion of fear since this is the secret to overcoming our sense of powerlessness, as is indicated from the following verse from the next chapter of Isaiah:

> *So do not fear, for I am with you; do not be dismayed, for I am your God. I will strengthen you and help you; I will uphold you with my righteous right hand.*

Isaiah 41:10

In these passages, fear is met with overwhelming power, not our power, but God's power. This is important since our power will never be sufficient to eliminate fear in our lives.

The writer of Hebrews takes this thinking to the next step in quoting God's promise to Joshua that, not only would God be his source of strength, but God would never leave him. This is the ultimate antidote to fear. If God possesses all power, and God has promised to strengthen me where I am weak, and God will never leave me, then I really have nothing to fear.

> God has said, "Never will I leave you; never will I forsake you." So we say with confidence, "The Lord is my helper; I will not be afraid. What can man do to me?"

Hebrews 13:5-6

Love

Power without love, however, is a terrifying prospect! Thankfully though, not only is God all-powerful, but He also loves us deeply. Love makes us comfortable in the power of God. As John says in the following passage, love drives out fear:

> There is no fear in love. But <u>perfect love drives out fear,</u> because fear has to do with punishment. The one who fears is not made perfect in love.

1 John 4:18

As we think of this dynamic involving fear and love, I am reminded of a scenario we have all seen many times. When a young child is frightened, where does the child tend to turn? Of course, for most children, they turn to their mother. Is this because their mother is all-powerful? No! It is because they sense their mother's love and her nature to protect her children. We are that child hiding behind mom, except we find our safe place in a loving God who loves us more than we could ever comprehend. This is the love demonstrated by God when He sent His Son to die for our sins in our place.

> *This is how God showed his love among us: He sent his one and only Son into the world that we might live through him. This is love: not that we loved God, but that he loved us and sent his Son as an atoning sacrifice for our sins.*

1 John 4:9-10

Love gives us the confidence that God's overwhelming power will further God's perfect will for our lives and bring us closer to Him.

Self-Disciplined Mind

Many of the things we fear are irrational or extremely unlikely. How often do we worry about things that never happen? Keeping our mind from racing ahead and entering into an endless list of "What ifs?" is difficult, but essential to overcoming our fears. This requires that we discipline our thinking. We cannot allow our minds to run rampant with speculation about things that may never happen, and in the process, paralyze us with fear.

Remember, we have already acknowledged that based on the power and love of God, we have nothing to fear. So those thoughts that would lead us back into fear are, in the words of the next verse, "set up against the knowledge of God." These thoughts must be taken captive.

> *We demolish arguments and every pretension that sets itself up against the knowledge of God, and <u>we take captive every thought</u> to make it obedient to Christ.*

2 Corinthians 10:5

Mental discipline requires us to control where our minds are going and focus on those thoughts that produce resilience and not focus on things that imprison us in fear. This is very different than mere "positive thinking," which often admonishes us to stay positive in spite of evidence to the contrary. The apostle Paul provides a great roadmap to this kind of disciplined thinking in the following verses from his letter to the Philippian church:

Do not be anxious (fearful) about anything, but in everything, by prayer and petition, with thanksgiving, present your requests to God.
And the peace of God, which transcends all understanding, will guard your hearts and your minds in Christ Jesus.
Finally, brothers, whatever is true, whatever is noble, whatever is right, whatever is pure, whatever is lovely, whatever is admirable—if anything is excellent or praiseworthy—think about such things.

Philippians 4:6-8

Whenever we begin to give in to fear, anxiety or worry, God provides clear instructions for dealing with those thoughts that rob us of our peace:

- We are to honestly present our concerns to God. Don't worry; He can handle it!

- We are to be thankful for the times in the past when God has been there for us. This will give us confidence in our current trial.

- We are to claim God's promise of peace that is far above anything we can imagine. This peace does not depend on the absence of conflict or perfect circumstances in our lives. It is a peace given by God, often in the midst of chaos or crisis.

- We are to discipline our thoughts, focusing only on those things that are constructive or Godly and not on imagined fears.

Questions for Thought and Discussion

1. What are some things in your life that you see as too fearful, that need to move from an outer zone to the challenge zone or even the comfort zone?

2. How do you respond to fear? Which face of fear is most common for you?

3. What are some things we can do to remind ourselves of God's power in fearful situations?

4. How can God's love move you to courage?

5. When are you most tempted to spiral into the fearfulness of "Whit if" thinking? How do you plan to discipline your mind in these moments?

Enemies of Resilience
Guilt

When we face a crisis, and need to be able to respond accurately to the problem, guilt and our response to past failures can make a significant difference in our level of resiliency. There are two opposite responses to guilt that are both damaging to our resilience. Some seek to place blame for their failures on others, while others may take responsibility for things beyond their control leading to shame. Both of these extremes, as we will show, result in our being less resilient in life.

Guilt Deflected Outward – Blame

One common response in the face of a crisis or setback is to direct blame away from ourselves and toward others. The temptation to blame others is easy to understand. If we can lay the blame on someone else, then we can feel good about ourselves and justify our own decisions, since whatever happens, "It's not my fault!" Consider some of these examples of the distortion of blame:

- Some people have such fragile egos that they feel they cannot ever accept responsibility or "blame" for a mistake. Their first response is to look for someone else to be at fault for whatever has happened.

- Others have come to see themselves as perpetual victims. Because they never accept personal responsibility for their mistakes and bad things keep happening to them, they assume they are always the victim of others in their lives.

- Some may also see blame simply as a way to avoid negative consequences. Whenever they find themselves in trouble, they transfer the blame along with the consequences to someone else while they walk away seemingly unscathed.

Assumptions:

The person who employs the blame distortion is often making one or more of the following erroneous assumptions:

- Some assume that accepting responsibility for a failure equates to weakness and makes them a failure. They want to be seen as always right and never at fault when things go wrong. This assumption is far from reality as we recognize that none of us are perfect. It is, however, easier to admit imperfection when we are being general than when we are getting specific about our faults.

- The victim mentality also assumes that all those around us are determined to see us fail or are taking advantage of us. This results in not trusting others.

Dangers:

- When we refuse to accept blame for those things we should be responsible for, we also delude ourselves and are no longer viewing the world as it really is. The Bible says, *"If we claim to be without sin, we deceive ourselves and the truth is not in us."* (1 John 1:8) Blaming becomes a tool of self-deception that nothing is wrong with us.

- The victim mentality, in addition to probably not being consistent with reality, creates a mistrust of others and destroys relationships that could be potentially helpful to our resilience. No one wants to be around someone who blames all their problems on others. Eventually, you get tired of being blamed.

- The biggest danger of the blame distortion is that if the problem is someone else's fault, then there is no reason for us to change anything we are doing to solve the problem. As long as we blame others, it will be up to others to fix the problem. You can never solve a problem you do not own first.

The Truth:

The reality is that all of us fail and the Bible teaches that "All have sinned and fall short of the glory of God" (Romans 3:23) Refusing to accept responsibility simply leads to repeated failures.

Failure, however, does not mean that we are any less capable of being used by God. In fact, the basic theme of Scripture is a story of redemption and forgiveness for our failures. John writes, "If we confess our sins, he is faithful and just and will forgive us our sins and purify us from all unrighteousness." (1 John 1:9)

An Example from Scripture:

In the opening chapters of the Bible, we are told that God placed a man and a woman (Adam and Eve) in a perfect garden (the Garden of Eden) and gave them one rule to obey (They were not to eat of the tree of the knowledge of good and evil). When they eventually disobeyed God, God confronts them with their sin. Their first response is an attempt to blame someone else for their disobedience. Adam blamed Eve and Eve blamed Satan masquerading as a serpent.

God made it clear that they were responsible for their own decisions and each would suffer the consequences of their disobedience. Blame didn't work in the Garden of Eden, and it doesn't work for us either.

Taking Responsibility

So, what do we do if we find that we are guilty of blaming when we are confronted with personal guilt? Here are three important questions to address if you have this tendency to blame.

- Even if you are not fully responsible for a problem, how did you contribute to the problem?
  It is seldom true in a conflict that one party is completely at fault while the other is completely innocent. We need to be willing to accept our personal responsibility for our part of the problem.

- Why do you feel so compelled to assign blame to other people instead of taking personal responsibility?
  Some people are afraid that admitting any responsibility for failure is a sign of weakness. In reality, we are fooling no one, deceiving ourselves, and prolonging the problem.

- How has blaming kept you from solving problems and being resilient in the past?
  As you look honestly at your past, can you recognize times that blame has kept you from addressing problems that needed to be resolved.

Guilt Reflected Inward – Shame

Shame is the opposite of blame, which, instead of deflecting responsibility to others, accepts responsibility for things beyond our control or responsibility. You cannot be responsible for problems you could not have prevented. Examples of shame are:

- A victim of domestic abuse sees the abuse as their own fault because of minor mistakes or perceived offenses. Make no mistake, abuse is not the fault of the victim! It is the sin of the abuser.

- The family of an addict blames themselves for the addictive behaviors of their loved one. The addict is responsible for their own decisions in response to temptation. This distortion is a form of co-dependency and can keep the addict from seeking treatment and help.

Assumptions:

- This distortion often begins with a low sense of personal value that believes, "I'm such a loser, it must be my fault."

- This distortion makes the assumption that even the problems brought about by the decisions of others are somehow our personal responsibility.

Dangers:

- Confusing responsibility with feelings of empathy, sadness or regret leads a person to take responsibility for things they had no control of or had no reasonable way of preventing. We may even take responsibility for the mistakes others have made.

- In taking responsibility for things beyond our control we trap ourselves in an endless cycle of self-blame, seeing ourselves as the cause of another person's pain when that is clearly not true.

- Shame assumes that we are always at fault. We see even little mistakes as evidence we are flawed and unworthy. Shame further leads us to believe that even our attempts to do the right thing are either futile or hypocritical.

- These dangers ultimately lead to the person who should be taking responsibility not making the changes necessary to avoid their poor decisions in the future. If someone else is willing to take responsibility, they have nothing to fix.

- Ultimately, shame leads to a downward spiral of depression, abusive relationships, addiction, and sometimes, suicide.

The Truth:

In the book of Ezekiel, in the Bible, the prophet, recognizing that all sin bears a penalty of death makes this statement:

> *The one who sins is the one who will die. The child will not share the guilt of the parent, nor will the parent share the guilt of the child. The righteousness of the righteous will be credited to them, and the wickedness of the wicked will be charged against them. "But if a wicked person turns away from all the sins they have committed and keeps all my decrees and does what is just and right, that person will surely live; they will not die.*

> Ezekiel 18:20-21

This passage makes the concept of personal responsibility perfectly clear. God does not hold any of us responsible for the bad actions or decisions of others. This passage also makes clear the correct way for those sins to be addressed. The person truly responsible is to turn away from their sins in genuine repentance and God will surely forgive.

It is also perfectly acceptable to feel sadness over the decisions of others without assuming responsibility. Several Bible characters expressed grief and sadness over the disobedience of those they cared deeply about, including Jesus himself, but they did not blame themselves for the sins of others.

An Example from Scripture:

In the Gospel of John, Jesus meets a woman at the well in Samaria at midday. This was not the usual time of day for the women to come to the well, but this woman was probably an outcast among the other women due to her having had five husbands and living with yet another man. According to the custom of the time, it was very unusual for Jesus to speak with a woman, let alone, one with such a questionable past. Jesus doesn't shame her for her past but engages her in a discussion of spiritual matters. Confession and repentance are never focused on shaming the sinner, but on changing the direction of the sinner. God's forgiveness gives new life and a fresh start to the sinner regardless of their past. In the end, this woman was responsible for leading her entire village to believe in Jesus.

Overcoming Shame

It is important in overcoming shame, to understand the difference between self-esteem and self-worth. Self-esteem is how we feel about ourselves and is often influenced by the opinions of others and our present performance. Because these are both volatile, our self-esteem will often result in wild swings between exuberance and discouragement.

Self-worth is our value as a person. Every human being is created by God with great value. The psalmist said it this way:

> I praise you because I am fearfully and wonderfully made; your works are wonderful, I know that full well.

> Psalm 139:14

God demonstrated our value in sending Jesus to die for us. Your performance does not determine your value. It is critical that we focus on our value in the sight of God and not on esteem rooted in opinions and performance.

Be careful, also, to not engage in negative self-talk and generalizations. "Always" and "Never" are seldom true, but will usually lead us to shame.

Realize that perfection is unattainable. There will always be a difference between what we visualized and reality. This only means you are human, not that you have failed.

60

Guilt resolved – Confession, Repentance, and Forgiveness

Guilt is not always a bad thing. There are times that guilt points us to admitting we are wrong and need to seek forgiveness and change our direction. This is genuine guilt. It is guilt that can and must be dealt with if we are to move forward in life. Unresolved guilt can be a heavy burden to bear as David experienced in the Psalms:

> *When I kept silent, my bones wasted away through my groaning all day long. For day and night your hand was heavy upon me; my strength was sapped as in the heat of summer. Then I acknowledged my sin to you and did not cover up my iniquity. I said, "I will confess my transgressions to the LORD"— and you forgave the guilt of my sin.*

> Psalm 32:3-4

The Bible provides very clear instructions for dealing with genuine guilt. The first step, as David describes above, is to openly confess our sins to God. Confession is the prerequisite to receiving God's forgiveness and beginning the process of healing.

> *If we confess our sins, he is faithful and just and will forgive us our sins and purify us from all unrighteousness.*

> 1 John 1:9

Biblical confession is agreeing with God about the nature of our evil actions. It requires that we admit our failures to ourselves and to God and those we have wronged with our actions. True confession of sin never makes excuses for our sin. It acknowledges that what we have done is evil and there is no excuse for our evil decisions and actions.

The Bible also adds that along with confession that there must be a desire to change direction looking forward. This is expressed in the following verses on, what the Bible refers to as repentance.

Repentance is a turning away from one thing and turn to something else.

> He who conceals his sins does not prosper, but whoever confesses and renounces them finds mercy.

Proverbs 28:13

> Godly sorrow brings repentance that leads to salvation and leaves no regret, but worldly sorrow brings death. See what this godly sorrow has produced in you: what earnestness, what eagerness to clear yourselves, what indignation, what alarm, what longing, what concern, what readiness to see justice done. At every point you have proved yourselves to be innocent in this matter.

2 Corinthians 7:10-11

Repentance is a change of mind toward our sin that leads to a change of direction in the future. Repentance does not mean that we won't fail in the future, but that we will take actions to avoid the failures of the past as much as possible.

Misplaced Guilt – Guilt without Responsibility

The final problem we need to deal with when it comes to guilt, is, how do we handle feelings of guilt when we are not actually responsible for the problem. This is misplaced guilt. Misplaced guilt should more properly be called regret or sorrow for the actions of another.

We often assume guilt for the actions of a spouse, a child or other friend or family member, even though they are fully responsible for their own actions. The reality is that each one of us is only responsible for our own actions. We cannot be truly guilty for things we have not done. But, we still must deal with these false feelings of guilt. The first step is to separate true guilt (the things I am responsible for) from the misplaced guilt (the things I am not responsible for). The misplaced guilt can then be dealt with by trusting God to give us peace even when our feelings may condemn us.

> *This is how we know that we belong to the truth and how we set our hearts at rest in his presence: If our hearts condemn us, we know that God is greater than our hearts, and he knows everything.*

1 John 3:19-20

In summary, we must be willing to face true guilt in our lives without blaming or shaming and then allow God to liberate us from the feelings of guilt that are not our responsibility.

Questions for Thought and Discussion

1. Do you have more of a tendency toward blame or shame in response to feelings of guilt?

2. If you have a tendency toward blame, what is your motivation for blame? How do you plan to overcome this problem?

3. If your tendency is self-shame, why do you think that you do this? What do you need to change to overcome shame?

4. Are there things you have never really confessed to God? Are you willing to seek His forgiveness now?

5. How can you claim God's promise of forgiveness for things you have confessed to God and have been forgiven of?

Enemies of Resilience
Pride

Pride is a word that conjures thoughts that are either very positive or very negative depending on your experience. If you have ever had a parent or other person you respected say, "I'm so proud of you!" the feeling is overwhelmingly positive. On the other hand, if you have had to deal with someone who was arrogant and egotistical, your response is one of revulsion. How can a single word result in such diverse emotions?

Let me be clear, the Bible recognizes both the positive and the negative sides of pride, although the overwhelming emphasis is on the sinfulness of pride.

The good side of pride is seen when we show approval to those we love and take pride and recognize their accomplishments. Paul speaks of this good side of pride when he talks about boasting of what others are doing.

> We, however, will not boast beyond proper limits, but will confine our boasting to the sphere of service God himself has assigned to us, a sphere that also includes you. Neither do we go beyond our limits by boasting of work done by others.

2 Corinthians 10:13, 15

The ultimate, good form of pride is to take pride in God. It is, after all, God who is the source of all good things in our life, as we will see later.

But, "Let the one who boasts boast in the Lord." For it is not the one who commends himself who is approved, but the one whom the Lord commends.

2 Corinthians 10:17-18

However, much of what the Bible has to say about pride is about the sin of pride. It is one of the most commonly discussed sins in the Bible, and the Bible is very unambiguous about the seriousness and consequences of pride in our lives. Consider some of the things God's Word says about pride:

- God detests the proud.

   The LORD detests all the proud of heart. Be sure of this: They will not go unpunished.

   Proverbs 16:5

- God is opposed to the proud.

   But he gives us more grace. That is why Scripture says: "God opposes the proud but shows favor to the humble."

   James 4:6

- Pride goes before a fall.

   Pride goes before destruction, a haughty spirit before a fall.

   Proverbs 16:18

This isn't a very pretty picture of pride. We shouldn't be surprised by this. Consider how many of the following synonyms for pride have a decidedly negative connotation:

- Haughty
- Opinionated

- Egotistical
- Judgmental
- Arrogant
- Condescending
- Autocratic
- Stubborn
- Vain

None of these terms is seen as a positive character trait. Why is pride seen in such a negative light? What is so bad about pride? Let's take a look at some of the reasons Scripture gives for the danger of pride.

Pride Distorts Reality

One of the primary problems with pride is that it distorts reality. The reality is that everything we have, whether it be skills, abilities, intelligence, or material wealth comes ultimately from the hand of God.

> *Wealth and honor come from you; you are the ruler of all things. In your hands are strength and power to exalt and give strength to all. Now, our God, we give you thanks, and praise your glorious name... Everything comes from you, and we have given you only what comes from your hand.*

1 Chronicles 29:12-14

The importance of this principle cannot be overestimated. What the Bible is telling us is that since everything comes from God, we have nothing in which to take pride. Whether it is our wealth or the skills and abilities that enabled us to earn that wealth, it all is a gift from God's grace.

For this reason, we have no place to boast or take pride in our accomplishments, since, without God, we could not accomplish anything.

> This is what the LORD says: "Let not the wise boast of their wisdom or the strong boast of their strength or the rich boast of their riches, but let the one who boasts boast about this: that they have the understanding to know me, that I am the LORD, who exercises kindness, justice and righteousness on earth, for in these I delight," declares the LORD.

Jeremiah 9:23-24

This concept is the natural extension of the previous passage. It clearly identifies things like wisdom, strength, and riches as some of the things we cannot boast about. This is reality! To take credit for what God has provided is not consistent with reality.

Pride Leads to Self-Sufficiency

When we fail to properly acknowledge God, we are easily deceived into thinking that we are self-sufficient and no longer need God. Pride leads to a man-centered view of our world that has no room for God.

The problem with pride is that we begin to take credit for what God has done, and eventually, we no longer have a need for God. God warned His people about this danger as they prepared to enter the promised land. He wanted them to remember their God in the midst of their coming success and affluence.

> Be careful that you do not forget the LORD your God... Otherwise, when you eat and are satisfied, when you build fine houses and settle down... then your heart will become proud and you will forget the LORD your God, who brought you out of Egypt, out of the land of slavery.

This acknowledgement of God's provision is to temper our opinion of ourselves. Paul instructs the Romans to use good judgment in what they think of themselves and to be cautious of an inflated sense of our own importance.

> *For by the grace given me I say to every one of you: Do not think of yourself more highly than you ought, but rather think of yourself with sober judgment, in accordance with the faith God has distributed to each of you.*

Romans 12:3

This is not the same as thinking poorly of ourselves or a false, exaggerated sense of humility. It is a view of ourselves that is neither inflated or that fails to consider our incredible value before God.

Pride Results in Strife

It should be no surprise, that one of the consequences of an attitude of self-centered pride and arrogance is continual strife and conflict. Pride gets in the way of personal relationships. It puts our own interests ahead of others, creating a strain in the relationship. The writer of Proverbs, observes:

> *Where there is strife, there is pride, but wisdom is found in those who take advice.*

Proverbs 13:10

This strife results from self-focused nature of pride which fails to consider the needs or interests of others. When we engage in this focus only on our needs, conflict and strife are a natural consequence.

Often, an indicator of a problem with pride is found in the way we speak to others. Proverbs describes the speech of the proudful person as arrogant, a mocker and insolent fury.

> *Those who guard their mouths and their tongues keep themselves from calamity. The proud and arrogant person—"Mocker" is his name—behaves with insolent fury.*

> Proverbs 21:23-24

It is little wonder, that proud, arrogant speech would create a strain on relationships, creating the kind of strife and tension that makes resilience more difficult.

Consider what C.S. Lewis had to say about pride: "According to Christian teachers, the essential vice, the utmost evil, is Pride. Unchastity, anger, greed, drunkenness, and all that, are mere flea bites in comparison: it was through Pride that the devil became the devil: Pride leads to every other vice: it is the complete anti-God state of mind... it is Pride which has been the chief cause of misery in every nation and every family since the world began."[2]

Pride is an attitude of self-sufficiency, self-importance, and self-exaltation in relation to God and others. Toward God, it disregards and takes credit for what God has done. Toward others, it is an attitude of contempt and indifference. As C.S. Lewis observed, "Pride is spiritual cancer: it eats up the very possibility of love, or contentment, or even common sense"[3]

---

[2] C.S. Lewis, Mere Christianity (New York: Simon & Schuster Touchstone edition, 1996), 109, 111.
[3] Lewis, Mere Christianity, 112.

Solutions for Pride

We must stop comparing ourselves to others.

When we are proud, we are often guilty of comparing ourselves to others. The problem with this is that we are selective in comparing only those things in which we compare favorably, and we also tend to be completely blind to our own faults and shortcomings while seeing clearly the faults of others.

Jesus revealed the arrogance of this form of comparison when He told the story of the Pharisee and the tax collector in Luke 18. The Pharisees are introduced as those *"who were confident of their own righteousness and looked down on everyone else."* As this Pharisee comes to worship God, he prays in a loud voice dripping with arrogance and self-glorification, *"God, I thank you that I am not like other people—robbers, evildoers, adulterers—or even like this tax collector."* His choices for the objects of his comparison are clearly selected to inflate his self-righteousness.

By contrast, the tax collector, who no doubt had a dubious reputation based on the dishonest and abusive nature of tax collectors in the first century, comes to worship in complete humility.

> But the tax collector stood at a distance. He would not even look up to heaven, but beat his breast and said, 'God, have mercy on me, a sinner.'

> Luke 18:13

Jesus addresses, not only the effectiveness of their worship but also their future outlook:

> "I tell you that this man, rather than the other, went home justified before God. For all those who exalt themselves will be humbled, and those who humble themselves will be exalted."

Comparing ourselves with others is both the means and the evidence of a prideful and arrogant spirit.

We must continually develop a spirit of thankfulness.

One of the things that contributes to prideful thinking and is therefore, an important key to overcoming pride is our thankfulness to God. Thankfulness, by its very nature, gives credit to someone else. In this way, it is an important protection against pride. When we fail to express thankfulness, we are usually tempted to start taking credit for our accomplishments, and pride is just around the corner.

In the Old Testament, when Israel was preparing to enter the land God had promised them, God warned them about what would happen, if, in their newfound affluence, they failed to give God the proper credit for what He had done.

> Be careful that you do not forget the LORD your God, failing to observe his commands, his laws and his decrees that I am giving you this day. Otherwise, when you eat and are satisfied, when you build fine houses and settle down, and when your herds and flocks grow large and your silver and gold increase and all you have is multiplied, then your heart will become proud and you will forget the LORD your God, who brought you out of Egypt, out of the land of slavery... You may say to yourself, "My power and the strength of my hands have produced this wealth for me." But remember the LORD your God, for it is he who gives you the ability to produce wealth, and so confirms his covenant, which he swore to your ancestors, as it is today.
>
> Deuteronomy 8:11-14, 17-18

Notice, it is God who has given them the ability to produce wealth and to avoid the trap of pride, they must properly acknowledge Him. The simple act of thankfulness would acknowledge God's provision and their dependence on Him, while also protecting them from the trap of pride.

We must adopt the mind of Christ and cultivate humility.

As is often true in other areas, if we truly want to rid ourselves of pride, we must replace it with something else. The Bible is very clear about the alternative to pride. It is humility modeled after Jesus Christ.

> In your relationships with one another, have the same mindset as Christ Jesus: Who, being in very nature God, did not consider equality with God something to be used to his own advantage; rather, he made himself nothing by taking the very nature of a servant, being made in human likeness. And being found in appearance as a man, he humbled himself by becoming obedient to death—even death on a cross!

Philippians 2:5-8

Jesus had every right to be proud. Unlike us, He truly possesses unlimited power and knowledge. He is the God of the universe, but this passage tells us that He voluntarily gave up the exercise of what was rightfully His to become a man and die on the cross. Consider what it meant for Almighty God to accept all the limitations of humanity. He lived with these limitations for 33 years on earth and then allowed mere men, His own creation, to sentence Him to a horrible death on the cross. He did all of this out of love for us so that we could be forgiven for our sins. It is the ultimate example of humility, not looking out for our own interests, but considering the interests of others. It is this mindset that we are to adopt in the place of pride.

This mindset of humility will also result in very different relationships than are evidenced by pride. Where pride produces strife, humility produces harmony.

> Live in harmony with one another. Do not be proud, but be willing to associate with people of low position. Do not be conceited.

Romans 12:16

Pride is an incredibly destructive force that limits our resilience by keeping us from admitting mistakes, seeking help, or changing our lives, all in the name of arrogant pride.

Questions for Thought and Discussion

1. In your opinion, what is the greatest danger of pride? Why?

2. What are some of the problems with comparing ourselves to others?

3. How does thankfulness deter pride?

4. How is Christ's example of humility helpful to us in rejecting pride?

5. Can you think of examples when pride has created a lack of harmony in your relationships? Why is this important?

Enemies of Resilience
Addictions

Negative habits, addictions or even our customary responses to certain situations can often limit our ability to be resilient in a crisis. Everyone has these areas of their life that they know are, at best, not a positive force and more likely, are holding them back. Too often we see these areas as acceptable flaws that only confirm that we are "only human." Unfortunately, these are often, at least partially responsible for our failure to bounce back when misfortune strikes, and we need all our strength to fight back.

What follows in this chapter is not an exhaustive discussion of addictions. Many volumes have been written on this subject and the limited space in this chapter cannot address all the issues relating to addictions, but my desire is to point to some Scriptures that will provide a better understanding of some of the issues related to this difficult subject.

The Bible describes the struggle we all feel in these areas of our life where we don't seem to have control over our actions.

> *I do not understand what I do. For what I want to do I do not do, but what I hate I do... As it is, it is no longer I myself who do it, but it is sin living in me. I know that nothing good lives in me, that is, in my sinful nature. For I have the desire to do what is good, but I cannot carry it out.*

Romans 7:15-18

Whether it's an addiction to alcohol or drugs, or a nasty habit, we have all experienced this feeling of failure to win over something we know is destructive and contrary to the kind of life we really want to live. We make promises to ourselves and others, but we repeatedly stumble and fall, despite our best intentions. So, how do we achieve victory over difficult habits and/or addictions?

The Big Question: Why do you do it?

While it may be tempting to gloss over this question with simple answers, it is vitally important that we really understand our motivation for doing something we know is wrong or destructive even in the face of overwhelming evidence that we are messing up our own lives in the process. Physical addiction is only a small part of this answer. The real answer is that every addiction or habit provides something we want or need. The alcoholic may be seeking to forget painful memories or that habit may be a coping mechanism for dealing with stress or any number of other reasons. If we do not identify clearly and specifically what it is that we get from our addictive or destructive behavior, we will not be able to identify the means that will work for us to overcome the behavior. Without this answer, the rest of our efforts are useless and destined to fail.

The first step is to identify habits or addictions that are destructive or damaging in your life. This requires courageous honesty as we face our own shortcomings. What is a habit or addiction that you need to deal with to be more resilient?

Addictions can come in the form of both addictive substances (alcohol, drugs, etc.) or addictive behaviors (gambling, porn, eating disorders, or sex addictions).

Once you identify your need, it is time to think through the reasons you do the things you do despite the negative consequences in your life. There are many common reasons given for continuing to engage in addictive behaviors, including escape from reality, numbing a pain or lowering inhibitions to deal with social situations. Each person has unique reasons for their choices and must answer the question, "Why do you do it?" (Think about this answer)

As we think seriously about our response to this important question, our answer raises additional questions.

- Is our engaging in an addictive behavior keeping us from handling situations in a healthier way? Example: An alcoholic who drinks to escape from an unhappy marriage rather than work at improving the marriage.

- Is there a better way to get the "benefits" we seek from our addiction or habit without engaging in addictive behaviors? Example: Person who smokes cigarettes to avoid gaining weight rather than using diet and exercise to control weight gain.

- Are there other issues that are not being addressed because we are treating the symptoms of our real problem with our addiction? Example: Person suffering from a diagnosed mental condition or chemical imbalance whose addiction keeps them from getting the care and treatment they really need.

The answers to these questions will help to direct us as we seek a lasting solution to the problem of addictions and negative habits.

Four Causes of Dependency[4] (Why we do it)

1. Chemical imbalance – This can be brought on by a variety of sources and needs to be diagnosed by a medical professional.

2. Unresolved events from the past – Unresolved pain and hurts can leave us susceptible to addictions. This is the

---

[4] Chris Prentiss, The Alcohol and Addiction Cure, page 145

focus of this unit on the "Enemies of Resilience." Further counseling may also be helpful in this area.

3. Beliefs you hold that are inconsistent with what is true – This is the focus of the "Beliefs Matter" unit of this book which examines how our beliefs influence the decisions we make in life.

4. Inability to cope with current conditions – This inability to cope indicates a need for building a support team to assist in dealing with difficult situations. None of us can "go it alone."

What does the Bible say about Addictions?

Much of what the Bible says about addictions is addressed to alcohol abuse, but can easily be applied to other forms of addiction as well. Consider the following passages:

Woe to those who rise early in the morning to run after their drinks, who stay up late at night till they are inflamed with wine. They have harps and lyres at their banquets, pipes and timbrels and wine, but they have no regard for the deeds of the LORD, no respect for the work of his hands.

Isaiah 5:11-12

Wine is a mocker and beer a brawler; whoever is led astray by them is not wise.

Proverbs 20:1

What are the Effects of Addiction?

Addictions inevitably come at great cost, whether it be our physical health, finances, relationships, or our happiness, the toll is more than we ever expect. Whether substance abuse or addictive behaviors, addictions lead us away from what we need and want in life. Personal control is lost to the addiction. The following account from Proverbs describes the cycle of addiction and its consequences.

> *Who has woe? Who has sorrow? Who has strife? Who has complaints? Who has needless bruises? Who has bloodshot eyes? Those who linger over wine, who go to sample bowls of mixed wine. Do not gaze at wine when it is red, when it sparkles in the cup, when it goes down smoothly! In the end it bites like a snake and poisons like a viper. Your eyes will see strange sights and your mind imagine confusing things. You will be like one sleeping on the high seas, lying on top of the rigging. "They hit me," you will say, "but I'm not hurt! They beat me, but I don't feel it! When will I wake up so I can find another drink?"*

Proverbs 23:29-35

This passage begins with six questions about the negative consequences of addiction. Results such as woe, sorrow, strife, complaints, bruises, and bloodshot eyes point to the physical, emotional, and social results of addictions. With these outcomes, it is a wonder anyone would chance an addiction by engaging in the use of alcohol, drugs or destructive behaviors.

The author next considers the lure of addiction. All addictions have an initial appeal that draws us in. The taste of our favorite drink, the "high" of the alcohol or drugs, the "fun" of things like porn or gambling, all seem pleasurable and safe at first. It is only later that we reap the consequences of our addiction.

Proverbs then goes on to describe the "bite" of addiction. What went down smooth is now poison. Our perceptions of reality are altered and unreliable. We even go as far as to be impervious to pain and the risk of dangerous situations we would normally avoid if sober. Despite all of this, as our addiction takes control, our every waking thought is consumed with feeding our addiction.

As you can see from these passages, the Bible clearly warns against being controlled by addictions and substance abuse. The Bible also has a lot to say about how we should deal with the addictions that threaten to control our lives.

Why are We So Powerless in the Face of Addiction?

The Bible recognizes that our natural tendencies taken to extremes will result in destructive and addictive behaviors. Part of the human condition is that ever since the Garden of Eden, man has had a bent or tendency toward sin. This is called our sinful nature. This becomes our default mode and it is a constant pull toward sin and destruction. Here is how the Bible describes this sin nature.

> *The acts of the sinful nature are obvious: sexual immorality, impurity and debauchery; idolatry and witchcraft; hatred, discord, jealousy, fits of rage, selfish ambition, dissensions, factions and envy; drunkenness, orgies, and the like. I warn you, as I did before, that those who live like this will not inherit the kingdom of God.*

Galatians 5:19-21

This explains the sense of being powerless over sin. We truly do not have the ability in ourselves to overcome our addiction. Sin and its destructive tendencies is our default mode.

How do We Find Power to Overcome Addiction?

We need God's help to overcome these destructive behaviors by replacing them with the character traits that are a result of our relationship with God. When we put our trust in God, we become a new creation with a new life and a new source of power for living a life free of addictions.

> *Therefore, if anyone is in Christ, he is a new creation; the old has gone, the new has come!*

2 Corinthians 5:17

God does a creative work in our lives giving us a fresh opportunity for a new life. This, however, does not mean that there is nothing for us to do. We must give God's Spirit control in our lives.

Do not get drunk on wine, which leads to debauchery. Instead, be filled (or controlled) with the Spirit.

Ephesians 5:18

It is only as we yield control over our life choices to God that we find freedom and victory in life. But, how do we give God control in our lives? We must constantly, moment by moment, decide whether to give control to our sinful nature or give control to God's Spirit.

So I say, live by the Spirit, and you will not gratify the desires of the sinful nature. For the sinful nature desires what is contrary to the Spirit, and the Spirit what is contrary to the sinful nature. They are in conflict with each other, so that you do not do what you want.

Galatians 5:16-17

What does God want to put in place of My Addiction?

If we are to be successful in fighting our addictions, we must replace our reliance on the sinful nature with a reliance on the Spirit which will then have the effect of radically changing the decisions we make

But the fruit of the Spirit is love, joy, peace, patience, kindness, goodness, faithfulness, gentleness and self-control. Against such things there is no law. Those who belong to Christ Jesus have crucified the sinful nature with its passions and desires. Since we live by the Spirit, let us keep in step with the Spirit.

Galatians 5:22-25

Notice that these characteristics are not achieved by our efforts but are the natural result of dependence on the Spirit. Many of the characteristics listed in this passage are also things we sought in our addictions:

- We look for love in sexual relationships, only to feel empty and alone.

- We look for happiness and joy in a party lifestyle, but the party always ends.

- We look for peace in a bottle or a pill, only to be enslaved by it.

The reality is that these desired outcomes are actually side effects of a relationship with God. We only find these things in obedience to our Creator and His plan for our life.

Is Addiction Ever Hopeless?

This battle is not easy, and no one will perfectly follow God's will for their life. There may yet be times of failure or relapse, but God provides hope, even in these hard times. God promises his forgiveness and restoration even when we repeatedly fail Him. God's love and forgiveness are unending!

> *Blessed is the one whose transgressions are forgiven, whose sins are covered. Blessed is the one whose sin the LORD does not count against them... I acknowledged my sin to you and did not cover up my iniquity. I said, "I will confess my transgressions to the LORD." And you forgave the guilt of my sin.*

> Psalm 32:1-2, 5

God works powerfully in our lives, even when we don't have the strength to go on. The Bible teaches that God lives in us and His power is able to do what we cannot do.

Now to him who is able to do immeasurably more than all we ask or imagine, according to his power that is at work within us, to him be glory in the church and in Christ Jesus throughout all generations, for ever and ever! Amen.

Ephesians 3:20-21

No person is beyond God's help! No addiction is ever unbeatable! No situation is ever hopeless!

Questions for Thought and Discussion

1. What is a habit, addiction or problem that you struggle with?

2. What is the attraction of the habit or addiction that leads you to engage in it despite negative consequences?

3. How has this habit or addiction negatively affected you or kept you from being resilient?

4. If our natural tendency is to sin, how do we practically overcome this power over us?

5. How does 1 Corinthians 10:13 help you to better understand the nature of temptation?

Beliefs Matter!

Beliefs → **Decisions** → **Outcomes**

Beliefs and Decision Making

Beliefs about Truth

Beliefs about Wisdom

Beliefs about Relationships

Beliefs about Temptation

Beliefs about Change

Beliefs and Decision Making

A crisis can come in many different forms. The situation is often not what we expected or at least desired, and it threatens to derail our plans and our hopes. How we respond to the crisis will usually determine whether this is a temporary detour or a life-destroying event. Some will look at the crisis and look for ways to mitigate the circumstances while others will be overwhelmed and despondent. What are the reasons for such drastic differences in the responses of people facing similar crises? This is an essential question to answer because if we can explain the reasons for the different responses, there is hope that we can help people to make more constructive and healthy responses in a crisis.

I believe that a large part of the difference between these ultimate outcomes is found in the belief system of the individual that influences and even determines the decisions they will make in a crisis.

Do Beliefs Matter?

Some would argue that personally held beliefs are merely a matter of personal preference and are neither, right or wrong, but merely an opinion about life. If we examine this position, however, we see quickly the fallacy of this belief. If I believe in something that is clearly not true, then the brutal consequences of reality will soon point out the weakness of my belief. As we consider this concept I would like to look at two Biblical characters to illustrate the influence of our beliefs on our eventual decisions and the actions we take based on those decisions.

Our first character is Saul, the first King of Israel. Saul had been selected as king of israel after the Israelites rejected God's rule through judges in favor of a king like their neighboring nations. Saul is quickly thrust into action in defending Israel from its neighbors, especially the Philistines. In 1 Samuel 13, we are told that the Philistines assembled a massive military force against Saul and his army. Saul desired the blessing of God as God had done for his predecessors, Moses, Joshua, and Samuel. His problem, however, is that God had instructed that only the priest was to offer the sacrifice to receive God's blessing and Samuel, the priest, was some distance from the front lines. This is how the Bible describes Saul's predicament:

> *When the Israelites saw that their situation was critical and that their army was hard pressed, they hid in caves and thickets, among the rocks, and in pits and cisterns. Some Hebrews even crossed the Jordan to the land of Gad and Gilead. Saul remained at Gilgal, and all the troops with him were quaking with fear. He waited seven days, the time set by Samuel; but Samuel did not come to Gilgal, and Saul's men began to scatter.*

1 Samuel 13:6-8

Faced with these circumstances, Saul begins to think through his options and rationalizes a response, deciding to offer the sacrifice himself, in direct disobedience to God. How did he come to this decision? I would like to outline what I see as the process by which Saul comes to his disasterous conclusion:

1. Saul believed that he needed God's blessing (nothing wrong, so far).

2. Saul believed that he was losing control of his troops (probably true).

3. Saul believed that God's blessing could be acquired by going through the motions of offering the sacrifice, even if he was in disobedience to God in offering the sacrifice (God's blessing is not a good luck charm. God blesses faithful obedience).

4. Saul believed that winning the battle was more important than strict obedience to God (big problem here).

It is interesting that as soon as Saul completes the offering of the sacrifice, Samuel arrives at the battle. Saul excuses his disobedience with this description of his thinking:

"When I saw that the men were scattering, and that you did not come at the set time, and that the Philistines were assembling at Mikmash, I thought, 'Now the Philistines will come down against me at Gilgal, and I have not sought the LORD's favor.' So I felt compelled to offer the burnt offering."

1 Samuel 13:11-12

Saul's belief that circumstances could override God's instructions led him to directly defy God. Before we condemn Saul too much, we should consider that we are often guilty of the same rationalization. We believe that our circumstances require us to make an exception to God's instructions. This belief leads to moral compromise and devastating consequnces.

The reality is that all of our decisions are rooted in our deeply held beliefs and once those beliefs change, so will the decisions based on those beliefs.

Our second Bible character is one of the major characters of the New Testament and the author of most of the Epistles, the Apostle Paul (originally named Saul until his name is changed after his conversion). Paul was the first missionary, taking the Gospel to most of the known world in his day, but he wasn't always an advocate of Christianity. In the book of Acts, Paul was an opponent of Christianity in his defense of Judaism. Paul himself later describes himself in these words:

If anyone else thinks he has reasons to put confidence in the flesh, I have more: circumcised on the eighth day, of the *people of Israel, of the tribe of Benjamin, a Hebrew of Hebrews; in regard to the law, a Pharisee; **as for zeal, persecuting the church;** as for legalistic righteousness, faultless.*

Philippians 3:4-6

Notice, that among the reasons he would put confidence in himself is that "as for zeal (he) was persecuting the church." What would make anyone believe that persecuting others was a good thing? Simply put, because he thought he was right and they were wrong, he was justified in his actions to imprison and even kill his opponents.

From the crusades to Islamic terrorists and many other examples throughout history, we have often seen brutality and evil justified in the name of religion. In each instance, however, it is necessary first for the individual to believe that evil can be justified if the cause is right. Transformation of beliefs always precedes committing acts that one would at one time have considered abhorrent or unimaginable.

I would like to diagram this connection between our beliefs, decisions, and outcomes in the following simple diagram:

This diagram has several implications that need to be noted and acknowledged in order to benefit from understanding this connection.

Decisions do not come out of thin air; they are based on deeply held beliefs.

We all have a set of beliefs about how life works and what is important in life and those beliefs are revealed in our decisions. A teen who values being popular among his peers will make decisions that will reveal that priority. A person who deeply values honesty will tend to make decisions where that value of honesty is upheld.

Our beliefs and values are often revealed by the nature of our decisions.

This naturally follows the previous discussion. If my decisions are based on what I really believe, then, I can see what I really believe (as opposed to what I say I believe) by examining the decisions I have made. I may say that I love others, but if I am not demonstrating that by my decisions, there are serious questions about whether or not I truly believe what I profess to believe. It is possible to fool ourselves by intellectually accepting the truth of a belief while not really being willing to trust that belief enough for it to influence our decisions.

Our decisions influence or determine the outcomes we experience.

It is possible for a person to make a bad decision based on a faulty belief and get lucky enough to not experience the negative outcome. Consider the drunk driver who is able to get home safely despite his intoxicated state. It is also possible to make good decisions based on accurate beliefs and experience a negative outcome. While both of these scenarios are possible, it is more likely that the decision based on a defective or inaccurate belief will result in a bad outcome than is true for the good decision. The person who counts on betting at the track to fund his retirement is more likely to fail than the person who invests in sound investments even though there is no 100% guarantee.

Making a different decision without challenging the underlying belief will not fix the problem.

Most of the time when we encounter a bad outcome, we are inclined to look for how we can avoid that result in the future. This usually takes the form of deciding not to make that decision again. (This is only true if we recognize the previous concept that our decisions influence our outcomes. The person who refuses to take responsibility or admit to his part in producing the outcome is hopelessly doomed to repeating his mistakes.) The problem with just making a different decision is that the new decision is still based on the old belief and is likely to also be a bad decision.

Let me give you a personal example. When I was in second grade, I had a teacher who told me that I was stupid and would never be successful in school (So much for molding young minds to learn). For the next few years, I honestly believed she was right and my decisions, like goofing around in class and not doing homework, just confirmed her assessment of me. It wasn't until a man in my church took an interest in me and challenged that belief, that I would even consider the possibility that I could be successful in school. Beliefs are always the foundation for our decisions, and a different decision doesn't help if it is based on the same defective belief.

Belief in something which is not true can have dangerous consequences.

From the addict who believes he can manage his addiction and that "just one time" won't hurt, to the abused woman who believes she can be "good enough" to stop her abuser, to the teen convinced that she will be popular if only she compromises what she knows to be right, each is wrong and will be hurt badly because of their defective belief.

There is a way that seems right to a man, but in the end it leads to death.

Proverbs 14:12

Just because in the heat of the moment or from our distorted perspective something seems right does not make it right and the consequences can be life-altering. We need to be careful to evaluate our beliefs in the light of truth and in collaboration with Godly people who truly care about us. I have long advised that teens work through their responses to various situations they know they will face before the pressure is on and devise a planned response that is rooted in beliefs that are true and not on the emotion of the moment. Wrong beliefs lead to bad decisions and even worse outcomes.

Wrong beliefs can seem very logical

Have you ever argued a position you know is wrong but, nevertheless, you can construct a logical sounding argument to support your wrong decision? We probably all have done this at one time or another, especially during our teen years, but the fact that we can make something sound logical does not make it true. This is also important because many today have elevated opinions to the level of truth and once you accept that opinions equal truth you can argue virtually anything. The apostle Paul recognized that there were many worldly philosophies in his time that could enslave believers and so he provided them the following warning:

See to it that no one takes you captive through hollow and deceptive philosophy, which depends on human tradition and the basic principles of this world rather than on Christ.

Colossians 2:8

Notice that the difference between truth and enslaving error is the foundation of the beliefs. Hollow and deceptive philosophies are always based on the popular thinking of the world around us while truth is rooted in Christ.

Admitting our beliefs are wrong can be very difficult, but essential to experiencing different results

What do we do when we realize we have been wrong about something we believed and the reason for our bad decisions falls squarely at our own feet? While we may be tempted to cover it up or blame someone else, the Bible gives us a better solution. At the dedication of the newly built temple, God anticipated that His people would wander from God and find themselves in need of a course correction.

If my people, who are called by my name, will humble themselves and pray and seek my face and turn from their wicked ways, then will I hear from heaven and will forgive their sin and will heal their land.

2 Chronicles 7:14

In this passage, God gives us a step by step approach for dealing with our sinful decisions and none of them are necessarily easy. The first step is to humble ourselves. Isn't it true that we often continue to push on in a wrong direction simply because we are too proud to admit we are going the wrong direction? It takes humility to say those words, "I was wrong." Once we admit our error, we are directed to pray and seek God's face. This goes far beyond asking God to bless our future efforts. To "seek His face" is to earnestly desire to know and desire to follow God's direction. It is not only the admission that "I was wrong," but also the acknowledgement that "I don't know the answers myself." The final step in this process is to "turn from our wicked ways." This is proceeding, not in the same direction we were before, but going in an entirely new direction that is consistent with where God is leading us as we seek His face.

It is only when we have taken these important steps of confession and repentance that we become the beneficiaries of God's promises in this passage. God makes three promises to the repentant sinner:

- The first is that He will hear from heaven. This is the assurance that our prayer and our seeking God's face will be heard by Almighty God.

- Secondly, God promises to forgive our sins. God's forgiveness goes far beyond anything we have experienced in our forgiveness of others. God completely removes the penalty for our sins (although there may still be some natural consequences) and chooses to never hold our sin against us again.

- Lastly, God promises to "heal their (our) land." This is a complete restoration to holiness (completeness). God's work on behalf of the repentant sinner brings unimaginable hope in the midst of our failure.

Freedom is found only in believing the truth

The importance of basing everything we believe on truth (reality) and not just on what we wish to be true cannot be overemphasized. Beliefs that are based on personal opinions and questionable logic will always yield unacceptable results

Jesus said, "If you hold to my teaching, you are really my disciples. Then you will know the truth, and the truth will set you free."

John 8:31-32

Examples of beliefs that result in bad decisions and worse outcomes:

Defective Belief #1 - Our feelings and emotions should drive our responses and decisions

While most people would not admit that this is their basis for making decisions, it is extremely common for people to make decisions from the insignificant to the life-changing based solely on feelings and emotions. The problem is that feelings and emotions are often not consistent with reality and therefore are not a reliable basis for our decisions. We may feel invincible, but that doesn't mean we should engage in very risky behaviors. We may feel financially well-off, but an emotional spending spree could quickly change things. Our feelings are often inconsistent with reality and when we depend primarily on emotions to make our decisions, or decisions are often bad decisions.

Defective Belief #2 - My problems are all the fault of others, bad luck, etc.

While we may occasionally be a victim of things beyond our control, many of our problems are the result of our own decisions. A failure to accept responsibility for our problems or attempting to always blame others for problems means that we will never even accept that we have a problem and will be unable to identify the defective beliefs that produced our bad decisions. The fact is that if you have a recurring problem, it probably isn't just bad luck or the fault of others, it could be you.

Even when we are victims, we can and must be resilient enough to overcome the circumstances and move on from the event. Accepting the role of helpless victim will never help us overcome the obstacles we face in picking up the pieces of our lives and moving ahead to a better life.

Defective Belief #3 - God is whatever I believe Him to be

People have many different beliefs about the existence of God, and if He exists, what He is like. This is a very important question for us to answer since it forms the basis for most of our other beliefs. We can argue from the viewpoint of our own opinions, but we are unlikely to come to much agreement. In reality, the most important question we must answer is "Does God exist?"

- If God exists, we cannot define Him. We can only discover who He is and what He desires. We can look at the world around us, how God has shown Himself throughout history and even look at how He has revealed Himself in the Bible.

- If God does not exist, it is foolish to create something in our minds that does not exist. In this case, God would be irrelevant because He would not be real.

- Either way, the one thing we cannot do is define a God of our own imagination. A self-created God is not God at all. It is idolatry.

Questions for Thought and Discussion

1. What are some of the sources of your beliefs? Which sources are you most and least confident of their accuracy?

2. What problems or bad decisions have you found recurring in your life? What beliefs form the foundation for the decisions you have made in the past?

3. Have you identified any beliefs that you suspect may be leading you to repeatedly make poor decisions? What are they and what are the true beliefs that need to replace the defective belief?

4. As you think about the examples of defective beliefs at the end of the chapter, are any of these beliefs you have accepted in the past?

5. What is one belief you need to change and how do you think your decisions and outcomes will change as a result?

Beliefs about Truth

Beliefs Matter!

Beliefs → Decisions → Outcomes

"What is truth?" That question was first asked by Pontius Pilate just before he compromised his better judgment and his conscience by sentencing Jesus to death on the cross despite having no evidence of any crime. In the centuries since Pilate's fateful decision, many others have tried in vain to shape the truth to fit their own desires and actions. The problem, of course, is that truth is not easily shaped into something else because truth is at its essence that which is real and reality is not malleable. In our daily lives, knowing what is really true is essential given that our beliefs about what is true form the basis for our decisions, which in turn, produce the outcomes that define our life. The big question we must all resolve is this:

Is truth absolute and unchanging or...

Does truth depend on the individual and the circumstances?

In most areas of our lives, we acknowledge the concept of absolute (always true) truth. For instance:

1 foot = 12 inches

1 pound = 16 ounces
1 hour = 60 minutes
1 dollar = 100 cents

We recognize that any deviation from what is true is a lie and cannot be believed. However, when it comes to our moral and ethical decisions, we think that none of the rules apply to us.

We often think that circumstances and personal feelings impact the reality of our moral decisions.

- We may believe that it is wrong to lie, but in our circumstances, we justify telling a lie that benefits us.

- We want our spouse to be faithful, but when the temptation to cheat presents itself, we compromise our values.

- We are critical of things like anger, stealing, gossip or selfishness in others but are not bothered by those same shortcomings in ourselves.

Jesus defined the problem in the following passage from the Gospel of John:

This is the verdict: Light has come into the world, but men loved darkness instead of light because their deeds were evil. Everyone who does evil hates the light, and will not come into the light for fear that his deeds will be exposed. But whoever lives by the truth comes into the light, so that it may be seen plainly that what he has done has been done through God."

John 3:19-21

Why do we sometimes have trouble with drawing the lines between truth and lies, right and wrong, or light and darkness?

The reality is that we prefer a subjective standard of truth that depends on personal interpretation or individual opinions instead of a standard of truth. We prefer this because we know our actions are not consistent with the truth and rather than be revealed as a hypocrite, we prefer to believe the lie.

The popularity of "relative truth" which varies in relation to our opinions and preferences allows us to adopt virtually any belief and at the same time protects us from critics who would poke holes in our beliefs. If everyone can freely define their own definition of truth, then no belief is better than any other belief.

Four Truths About Truth

As we examine our understanding of truth, there are certain "truths" that we must acknowledge based solely on the definition of truth.

1. Truth is always consistent with reality. If it is real, it is also true. If it demonstrably not real, it cannot be true. It is essential that we understand this vital link between what is real and what is true.
   When my children were young, we would frequently play a game we called "Real or Pretend?" The object was for the kids to learn to discern which characters or situations were real and which were fictional stories for our entertainment. When we separate truth from reality, we find ourselves living in a fantasy that will someday come crashing down around us because... Reality Always Wins!

2. We don't invent or create truth. We discover it. This follows naturally from the previous statement. Truth is always consistent with reality, the way things are, not the way we want things to be. We can try to redefine the truth but that doesn't change the underlying reality, therefore we cannot create or define truth.
   Discovering truth requires a search for the evidence of the

truth and the willingness to accept the conclusions even if they are contrary to our preferred version of the "truth."

3. Our understanding of truth may change, but truth itself is unchanging. This is the reason that sometimes, accepted truths seem to change. It is not so much that truth has changed, but that new information has revealed the fallacy of what we believed to be true. Most of the world once believed the world was flat. The truth was that the earth was always round. When evidence was discovered that ran counter to the prevailing understanding, smart people recognized the truth.

4. The truth does not depend on how strongly or sincerely we believe something to be true. Our belief in something does not make it true. It is true whether or not we believe it to be true. You are free to believe that which is not true, but that does not make it true. It only makes you a fool for believing the lie. The reality is that feeling something is true is not the same as it being factually true. This truth is especially difficult for many people to accept since it requires us to acknowledge that something we felt very strongly about was in fact, not true.

What happens when we have beliefs that are not true or rooted in reality? The Bible describes the dilemma of belief in that which is not true in the following passage of Scripture:

They exchanged the truth of God for a lie, and worshiped and served created things rather than the Creator—who is forever praised.

Romans 1:25

The exchange of truth for a lie results in a misplaced trust. Instead of trusting God, the Creator, we redirect our trust to created things including our own distorted definition of the truth.

The rest of this chapter describes the inevitable descent into sin and destruction that results from replacing truth with a lie.

Discerning the difference between the truth and a lie can often be difficult. With the explosion of information available to us and the ease of making anything look good, more and more people are being led astray by lies posing as the truth. A generation ago, it was only possible to publish your ideas if you could find a publisher who would agree to publish your ideas. Today, anyone with an internet connection can influence the thinking of thousands or even millions without any critical analysis of their positions.

Furthermore, even usually reliable sources of information are sometimes unreliable and could lead us to believe things that are not true.

Consider the following sources of information, and for each one think about ways you have found it reliable and also times each one has proven to be wrong:

- The Internet
- Your Friends
- Popular media (music, TV, and movies)
- Books
- Teachers and authorities
- Your own feelings

While some of these sources may be more reliable than others, none are infallible, all can and have been wrong at one time or another. In this environment, it is difficult to develop a reliable standard for truth. Fortunately, God has not left us without clear instructions for knowing the truth. In the book of Proverbs, in the Bible, God warns us about relying on our own judgment and directs us to trust in God and the truth He has revealed to us in the Bible.

Trust in the LORD with all your heart and lean not on your own understanding; in all your ways acknowledge him, and he will make your paths straight. Do not be wise in your own eyes; fear the LORD and shun evil.

Proverbs 3:5-7

If we are at all honest with ourselves, we know that our own judgment and our understanding has often failed us. By acknowledging that we do not have all the answers, we allow for a higher source of information to guide us to the all-important truth. Proverbs says that this is God Himself. The next question is naturally, how do we discern what God says and how do we follow His path for us?

When Jesus was on earth, His disciples heard His teaching firsthand, and as they followed His teaching, they had the benefit of the wisdom and understanding of God in their search for truth. Here is what Jesus said about His teaching and the pursuit of truth:

Jesus said, "If you hold to my teaching, you are really my disciples. Then you will know the truth, and the truth will set you free."

John 8:31-32

Notice that in this verse, the source of the truth is found in holding to Jesus' teaching. I believe this means not only believing His teaching but also living out the truth we find in His teaching and then "the truth will set you free." It is not enough to have an intellectual agreement with Jesus' teachings; they must be the guide for our life. The Psalmist expresses this desire to live a life guided by devotion to living life God's way:

Show me your ways, O LORD, teach me your paths; guide me
in your truth and teach me, for you are God my Savior, and my
hope is in you all day long.

Psalm 25:4-5

So how do we discover God's truth? While it is true that we can learn about God in many ways, our primary source for truth is found in the Bible. The Bible is the record of God's dealings with men and the self-revelation of God. While God used about 40 human authors to create the Bible, He supervised the writing and preserving of the Bible. In its pages, we also find the historical record of God becoming man in the person of Jesus Christ. By examining the Biblical record of God's Word and the life of Jesus as it is recorded in Scripture, we can truly know the truth.

Some would argue that while the Bible was true at one time, that times have changed and what may have been true when the Bible was written, is no longer true. The problem with this belief is that it also requires God to change. If God is perfect and God changes, then God can no longer be perfect. Truth is what is like God; falsehood is that which is not like God.

Every good and perfect gift is from above, coming down from
the Father of the heavenly lights, who does not change like
shifting shadows.

James 1:17

Why is it important that God does not change? Think about it, if God could change, then everything we know and trust about God could change. This would include things like His love for us or His mercy, even His forgiveness of our sins. This would place us in a precarious situation of uncertainty. Fortunately for us, one of God's characteristics is that He is unchanging and we can take confidence in all that He says is truth.

The truth is an invaluable asset defining the correct decision to make in all areas of life. The writer of Proverbs reflected on the value of truth and came to this important conclusion:

Buy the truth and do not sell it; get wisdom, discipline and understanding.

Proverbs 23:23

Truth is essential to our ability to be resilient. It is critical to life itself!

Questions for Thought and Discussion

1. What are some "gray areas" where you have failed to distinguish clearly between right and wrong?

2. How do the four truths about truth, presented in this chapter, challenge some of your beliefs?

3. What are some reasons we tend to question Biblical truth as authoritative in our lives?

4. How can you better allow the truth of Scripture to be the authority in your decisions?

5. How have your beliefs about absolute truth impacted your ability to be resilient in the past?

Beliefs about Wisdom

It stands to reason that wise decisions will be better decisions and have better outcomes than impulsive, uninformed decisions. In virtually every area of life, most decisions present us with multiple options. There are some options we know would be a poor decision, but how do we make choices when the options aren't quite as clear? How do we separate the acceptable decision from the best decision? We describe this ability to discern the best decision as wisdom. While all of us would like to think we are wise, our track record often betrays a serious lack of good judgment. How can we consistently make better, wiser decisions?

The Most Important Question!

As we make decisions in life, one of the things that betrays a flawed belief system is the questions we use in the process of making our decisions. For many people, the primary question we ask ourselves is:

What do I want to do?

This question leads to decisions which are often emotional, impulsive and focused only on the immediate circumstances. This question also centers the decision on our own interests in the moment, resulting in self-centered decision making that disregards others around us and fails to consider broader consequences. Instead of this question, Biblical beliefs would instead ask the question:

What is the wise thing to do?

This question evaluates the decision from an entirely different perspective and requires that we consider the potential impact of our decisions. This question considers impacts beyond ourselves or the immediate future and considers far more alternatives that will often have a more beneficial impact for us and for others in terms of the eventual outcomes. We can further clarify this question with the following variations on this important question:

In light of my past experiences and decisions, what is the wise thing to do?

All of us have different pasts, different experiences, and different strengths and weaknesses. Those strengths and weaknesses mean that what may be wise for one person may not be wise for another. Things in our past such as an addiction, a failed relationship, a personal failing, or other area of weakness may mean that certain decisions that would be acceptable for others would be unwise given our past experiences.

In light of my current circumstances, what is the wise thing to do?

Our present circumstances can also dictate a different course of action. Sometimes the timing of a decision leads us to respond differently than we would at a different point in our life with different current circumstances. Financial resources, family needs, career directions can all be considerations that would make some decisions unwise.

In light of my future hopes and dreams, what is the wise thing to do?
We all have different dreams for the future, and sometimes those dreams require that we make different decisions in the present so that in the future we can do what we really want to do. The reality is you never want to trade what you want the most in your future for what you want in the moment.

Wise decisions will also consider the moral consequences of the decision and will always look for God's will in the decision. The wise decision will never be an immoral or unethical decision that would displease God. While God may sometimes use evil people to accomplish His purposes, He never designs for His people to do evil to accomplish His will. According to Paul in Ephesians, the evil decision is always unwise and foolish.

> *Be very careful, then, how you live—not as unwise but as wise, making the most of every opportunity, because the days are evil. Therefore do not be foolish, but understand what the Lord's will is.*

> Ephesians 5:15-17

The book of Proverbs has a great deal to say about wisdom and the lack of wisdom. In the book of Proverbs, written by King Solomon, there are three terms used for people who are lacking wisdom.

The Simple

This is one who is naive or lacking in knowledge and experience. The reality is that at one time all of us were simple and needed to grow in wisdom and judgment. Over time, hopefully, we learned what was wise and what was unwise. The simple person is often associated with youth and inexperience.

I saw among the <u>simple</u>, I noticed among the young men, a youth who lacked judgment.

Proverbs 7:7

The simple person is also seen as gullible and easily influenced by others as opposed to thoughtful and deliberative.

A <u>simple</u> man believes anything, but a prudent man gives thought to his steps.

Proverbs 14:15

The simple person also fails to look ahead and consider the consequences of their actions. They respond impulsively with little thought to the future, only the immediate circumstances

A prudent man sees danger and takes refuge, but the <u>simple</u> keep going and suffer for it.

Proverbs 22:3

In our youth, all of us made decisions that weren't very wise as we look back at our lives. The cure for our simple minds was to learn from our mistakes and gain experience that would protect us from those kinds of decisions in the future

The Fool

This person is one who knows what to do but doesn't care or rejects the right choice. Unlike the simple person, this person makes a deliberate choice to do what they know to be unwise. Most of us would be offended to be called a fool, yet by our actions, we fit the biblical definition of a fool. Consider some of the things in the following verses from Proverbs that describe the decisions of a fool

The way of a fool seems right to him, but a wise man listens to advice. A fool shows his annoyance at once, but a prudent man overlooks an insult.

Proverbs 12:15-16

He who trusts in himself is a fool, but he who walks in wisdom is kept safe.

Proverbs 28:26

A quick-tempered man does foolish things, and a crafty man is hated.

Proverbs 14:17

A fool finds pleasure in evil conduct, but a man of understanding delights in wisdom.

Proverbs 10:23

A fool finds no pleasure in understanding but delights in airing his own opinions. A fool's lips bring him strife, and his mouth invites a beating. A fool's mouth is his undoing, and his lips are a snare to his soul.

Proverbs 18:2,6-7

As we look at just these verses, we can compile quite a list of foolish tendencies:

- Fools act impulsively, doing whatever seems right.

- Fools do not listen to advice but, instead, are annoyed by the advice of others.

- Fools trust only in themselves and their own under-standing of a problem or situation.

- A fool finds pleasure in things that are evil

- A fool is more interested in airing his own opinions than in learning and understanding.

- A fool's mouth frequently gets him in trouble, even inviting a beating at times

- A fool finds his speech is even a detriment to his own soul (his spiritual life and relationship with God)

If any of these descriptions sound particularly convicting to you, you just might be what the Bible refers to as a fool.

One of the consequences of being a fool is that we often hurt those closest to us with our foolish decisions. It is the reason most of us would not want our children spending time with people making bad decisions.

> *He who walks with the wise grows wise, but a companion of fools suffers harm.*

> Proverbs 13:20

Where the simple man can be cured by time and more experience, the fool is much more difficult to cure. In order to be wise, the fool must decide to seek wisdom rather than continue their foolish ways, and most fools aren't about to admit they have been wrong. Sadly, for most fools, the cure for their foolishness is when God allows tragic consequences to come into their life, getting their attention and humbling them to the point they are ready for change.

The Mocker

The mocker is one who rejects wisdom and lashes out at those who would choose wisdom. This person goes beyond even the fool and demands that those around him also participate in his foolishness. When someone fails to follow their lead, the mocker will strike out with cruelty to punish those who desire to demonstrate wisdom. Consider the following descriptions of the mocker from the book of Proverbs.

A mocker resents correction; he will not consult the wise.

Proverbs 15:12

"Whoever corrects a mocker invites insult; whoever rebukes a wicked man incurs abuse. Do not rebuke a mocker or he will hate you; rebuke a wise man and he will love you.

Proverbs 9:7-8

Drive out the mocker, and out goes strife; quarrels and insults are ended.

Proverbs 22:10

- The mocker resents being corrected and will never consult others for advice.

- The mocker insults, abuses and hates anyone who rebukes or disagrees with him.

- A mocker is always accompanied by endless strife, quarrels, and insults.

- The only cure for those who are associated with a mocker is to drive them out of your life.

It is interesting that we find all three of these unwise responses in the questions of the following verse:

"How long will you <u>simple</u> ones love your simple ways? How long will <u>mockers</u> delight in mockery and <u>fools</u> hate knowledge?

Proverbs 1:22

It is clear that being simple, foolish or a mocker will never result in wise decisions and fruitful outcomes or a more resilient life.

How Do We Become Wise?

So what do we do if we think that we are guilty of unwise decisions and behaviors? What does it take to be wise? Proverbs also has a great deal to say about being wise, and one foundational principle is that it all begins with our attitude towards God:

> "The fear (awe or respect) of the LORD is the beginning of wisdom, and knowledge of the Holy One is understanding. For through me your days will be many, and years will be added to your life.
>
> Proverbs 9:10-11
>
> The fear of the LORD teaches a man wisdom, and humility comes before honor.
>
> Proverbs 15:33

In these verses, we see that wisdom begins with a proper respect for God. In respecting God, we are forced to humble ourselves and not see ourselves as having all the answers. This is the beginning of the journey towards true wisdom. Once we have a proper respect for God and are humble enough to know we need help, we are ready for the next step in gaining wisdom.

One difference between the wise and the unwise that is frequently repeated throughout the book of Proverbs and throughout Scripture is the ability to listen to advice and correction! No one enjoys being corrected, and some see asking for advice or instructions as a form of weakness. The reality is that seeking and following good and Godly advice will save us an immense amount of heartbreak in life.

He who listens to a life-giving rebuke will be at home among the wise. He who ignores discipline despises himself, but whoever heeds correction gains understanding.

Proverbs 15:31-32

Listen to advice and accept instruction, and in the end you will be wise. Many are the plans in a man's heart, but it is the LORD's purpose that prevails.

Proverbs 19:20-21

Wisdom begins in humbly accepting the advice of others. It is important that this advice come from those who have demonstrated wise, Godly counsel and that the advice is tested to ensure that it is consistent with the truth of God's Word.

The Components of Wisdom

The book of Proverbs uses several terms in the process of instructing us in wisdom. Knowledge, understanding, and discernment are all essential to attaining wisdom.

Knowledge – This involves having enough information to make a decision. For example, it is impossible to fix a car that isn't running until you gather enough information to diagnose the problem. Lack of enough information often leads us to make unwise decisions. Be sure you have all the facts.

Understanding – Information alone is not enough. We also need to understand the how and why behind the information. Understanding is the ability to draw the right conclusions from the facts available. In our analogy of a car repair, this would be the understanding of how automotive systems work so that the fact we gather lead to a meaningful and accurate diagnosis and a repair plan for the problem.

Discernment – Not all of the information we receive is true or reliable. We need to be careful to consider the source of our information and compare it to what we know to be true. Information that is not consistent with what we know to be true can lead us in the wrong direction. In our car example, an inaccurate gauge or erroneous instructions could lead to failure to repair the problem we wish to solve.

Wisdom – The application of knowledge, understanding, and discernment in our life choices.

Finally, wisdom must be reflected in our decisions and our actions to be effective. It is not enough to know the right answer if we fail to follow through with wise life choices.

> Who is wise and understanding among you? Let him show it by his good life, by deeds done in the humility that comes from wisdom.

James 3:13

Wisdom must also extend to all areas of our lives. It is very possible to be wise in one area of your life and foolish in other areas of your life. For example, a person may be very wise in his business decisions but foolish in his family relationships. For this reason, we must be constantly pursuing wisdom in all areas of our lives.

Answering the simple question, "What is the wise thing to do?" will always lead to better decisions and greater resilience in every area of our lives.

Questions for Thought and Discussion

1. Why is it more important to ask "What is the wise thing to do?" rather than "What do I want to do?"

2. As you look at some of your poorer decisions, would you say you tend to be more like the simple (naïve), the fool (rejecting truth), or the mocker (antagonistic to the truth)?

3. Humility is necessary for both submitting to God and accepting advise from others. Why do we (you) resist the humility required to be wise?

4. Among knowledge, understanding, and discernment, which is your greatest need in becoming wise?

5. Are there areas of your life where you tend to make consistently poor decisions?

6. How would asking the question, "What is the wise thing to do?" change the decisions and outcomes you have experienced?

7. How have your beliefs about wisdom impacted your ability to be resilient in the past?

Beliefs about Relationships

One area of our lives where we frequently make poor decisions is in our relationships with other people. These people could be family members, neighbors, co-workers, employers or friends. The consequences of these poor decisions can result in tension, arguments, the breakup of families or job loss. If it is important that we make good relationship decisions, it is critical that our beliefs about relationships are true, producing the outcomes we desire.

This is critical to our resilience because constructive and helpful relationships are often key to have a greater resilience in life. Being surrounded by caring people who help us to make good decisions is a valuable asset.

Consider for a moment the kinds of things we value in a close friend. What character traits would you look for in a friend? Now consider this:

- Are you the kind of person you would want as a friend?

- Are you the kind of employee you would hire for a job?

- Are you the kind of spouse or parent you would want to have?

The reality is that we often hold others in our lives to a higher standard than we have for ourselves and we are often blind to faults in our lives that we would readily point out in the lives of others.

In this lesson, we will look at what the Bible says about our beliefs regarding our relationships with other people, whether they be family, friends, co-workers or even enemies. We are going to look at five contrasts between the way most people treat others and what the Bible says about our personal relationships.

Loving vs. Selfish

"A new command I give you: Love one another. As I have loved you, so you must love one another.

John 13:34

This is one of the most frequent commands God gives us in Scripture. We are not only told to love others, but we are told to do it as God has loved us. While none of us can fully replicate the love God has shown us in our relationships with others, we are to seek to love others even when it costs us or when they fail to love us back.

Jesus told a story in Luke 10:30-37 to illustrate the kind of love we are to show for each other. He told of a man who was robbed and beaten along the road from Jerusalem to Jericho and was left bleeding and wounded. In time a priest passed by and instead of stopping to help the man, crossed to the other side of the road and went on his way. The priest surely would have known God's teaching about loving others and helping those in need, but for whatever reason, he chooses to not help the severely injured man. Next, we are told, a Levite passed the man. Levites were responsible for carrying out many of the routine tasks of the temple, one of which would have been caring for the poor and those in need. Although this man was clearly in need, the Levite chose to cross to the other side and go on his way.

Finally, a Samaritan man came upon the injured man. The relationship between the Jews and the Samaritans was long and complicated. Hundreds of years before Jesus lived, when the Israelites were taken into captivity first by Assyria and later the southern kingdom to Babylon, some Jews were left behind because they were not seen as being able to contribute to their captors. These people intermarried with the non-Jewish population and settled in Samaria. Furthermore, the Samaritans had developed their own places of worship which was seen as heretical by the Jews. When the Jews returned after their captivity, a strong hatred developed between the two groups of people rooted in racial, socio-economic and religious differences.

For this reason, it is quite surprising that the one person who stops to help the injured man is a Samaritan. We are told the Samaritan took pity on him, bandaged his wounds, treated his injuries and took him to the nearest inn, which would have been the best place for him to recover in a time before hospitals. The Samaritan then paid in advance for his lodging and even guaranteed payment for any additional expenses the innkeeper might incur.

Jesus had told this story by way of clarifying God's command to love your neighbor. An expert in the law had asked about who would qualify as a neighbor, clearly wanting a fairly restricted definition. Jesus' story and the accompanying question, "Which of these three do you think was a neighbor to the man who fell into the hands of robbers?" revealed that Jesus required a very broad definition of a neighbor as well as a very high standard of what it meant to "Love your neighbor."

While many would not have a problem demonstrating this kind of love toward those closest to them, and some would even extend this love to a needy stranger as in Jesus' story, few would take this as far as Jesus did. Jesus takes loving others even farther than just loving those who are close to us or those who are in need. Elsewhere in Luke's gospel, Jesus extends the command to love others even to our enemies

> *"But I tell you who hear me: Love your enemies, do good to those who hate you, bless those who curse you, pray for those who mistreat you. Do to others as you would have them do to you.*

Luke 6:27, 36

This love is not just how we should feel toward our enemies; it is translated into doing good to them, blessing them and praying for them. Verse 36, at the end of this passage, is often referred to as "The Golden Rule." It is important to understand that this applies not only to those closest to us but also to our enemies

We are too often more like the priest and Levite in the story, concerned primarily with our own interests, to genuinely love those who are hurting around us. A loving person, however, builds the respect and love of those around him as they see his concern for others. This kind of person will also be more resilient when trials come to him because of the deeper relationships he has cultivated.

Honest vs. Dishonest

The second most important belief for strong relationships is that of honesty. Whenever I ask about the traits people look for in a friend, one of the first mentioned is always honesty or integrity.

Every relationship requires an element of trust and trust is built through consistent and reliable integrity.

Often, when we compromise our integrity by doing something dishonest, we minimize it by seeing it as a little thing, but in the following passage, we see that the little things still define our level of honesty. If we can't be trusted in the little things, we can't be trusted in the big things either.

> "Whoever can be trusted with very little can also be trusted with much, and whoever is dishonest with very little will also be dishonest with much. So, if you have not been trustworthy in handling worldly wealth who will trust you with true riches? And if you have not been trustworthy with someone else's property, who will give you property of your own? "No servant can serve two masters. Either he will hate the one and love the other, or he will be devoted to the one and despise the other. You cannot serve both God and Money."

Luke 16:10-13

In personal relationships, betrayal of trust, even when we think of it as an insignificant issue, erodes trust in all areas of the relationship. There is no such thing as a little lie. For example, an employee who is dishonest in small things is likely also not to be trustworthy when the stakes are much larger.

Responsible vs. Irresponsible

Another important characteristic in building strong relationships is being responsible or faithful. The responsible person can be counted on to do what they say they will do. For example, as an employee, this person can be left to do a job, and they will work hard to complete the job. In family relationships, this person is one who keeps promises even when doing so is difficult or costly.

We have all been entrusted by God and the people in our lives with many things such as:

- Our possessions
- Our family
- Our jobs
- Our skills and abilities

Being responsible or faithful means that we manage well the things that have been entrusted to us.

> *Now it is required that those who have been given a trust must prove faithful.*

1 Corinthians 4:2

In my experience, faithfulness is usually tested in one of two ways:

- The first is when we think no one will notice that we have not followed through. When no one is watching, it is tempting to think that since no one will know, being unfaithful or irresponsible will have no consequences. Jesus described this scenario in Matthew 24:

> *"Who then is the faithful and wise servant, whom the master has put in charge of the servants in his household to give them their food at the proper time? It will be good for that servant whose master finds him doing so when he returns. I tell you the truth, he will put him in charge of all his possessions. But suppose that servant is wicked and says to himself, 'My master is staying away a long time,' and he then begins to beat his fellow servants and to eat and drink with drunkards. The master of that servant will come on a day when he does not expect him and at an hour he is not aware of.*

Matthew 24:45-50

As many cheating spouses, employees, or politician can no doubt attest, there is no such thing as a hidden sin. We may get away with it for a time, but sin is often exposed when we least expect it. Even when our sin is undetected, we need to realize that God sees everything we do and will someday bring it to light at the judgment.

- The second test of our faithfulness occurs when the cost of being responsible or of keeping our promises is greater than we are willing to pay. We are often unaware when we make promises or commitments of all that will be involved to follow through on our promises.

  For example, a couple makes a commitment when they get married to be faithful to one another, not knowing what the future will hold. It is, however, a lifetime commitment. There will be difficult times, but we are still to honor the promises we have made. It should be noted that keeping our commitment even when it is difficult, deepens the relationship and is even more rewarding.

Reputable vs. Deceptive

Reputations are also built on trust demonstrated by faithfulness over a long period of time. A good reputation is of great value, as it leads others to extend their trust based on the recommendations of others who have known you. It is just as true that a bad reputation can be hard to overcome and have damaging consequences.

A good name is more desirable than great riches; to be esteemed is better than silver or gold.

Proverbs 22:1

Reputations are usually created over long periods of time, even years. Reputations can also be destroyed, but by contrast, it often takes only a single act of deceit to destroy a good reputation and create a bad one.

> *A man of perverse heart does not prosper; he whose tongue is deceitful falls into trouble.*

Proverbs 17:20

A good reputation can bring great rewards in life, while a bad reputation presents obstacles and barriers to overcome. Rebuilding a reputation is difficult and will take considerable time because once trust is lost, it is not easily granted again. Nevertheless, it is critical to begin to build a good reputation as someone who can be trusted.

Hardworking vs. Lazy

Many people have bemoaned the loss in recent years of a work ethic in many places. Too many people have adopted a philosophy of doing the minimum to get by instead of giving their full effort. There are many justifications given for this from companies taking advantage of their workers to the lack of recognition for the extra effort. The Bible is clear that in everything we do, we are to give our all.

> *Obey your earthly masters in everything; and do it, not only when their eye is on you and to win their favor, but with sincerity of heart and reverence for the Lord. **Whatever you do, work at it with all your heart, as working for the Lord, not for men**, since you know that you will receive an inheritance from the Lord as a reward. It is the Lord Christ you are serving. Anyone who does wrong will be repaid for his wrong, and there is no favoritism.*

Colossians 3:22-25

We have all worked for a bad boss at one time or another. Often, the response to this kind of authority is one of being

125

uncooperative and unmotivated. According to this passage, however, we are to work as if we are working for Christ himself in those situations, giving our full effort. This is the secret to working in a bad work environment and not being overcome by the negativity of our surroundings.

The opposite of being hard working is to be lazy. This person seeks to avoid hard work and often has an expectation of entitlement that things will be given him. The Bible is blunt and clear about the outcome for this kind of person.

> *How long will you lie there, you sluggard? When will you get up from your sleep? A little sleep, a little slumber, a little folding of the hands to rest—and poverty will come on you like a thief and scarcity like an armed man.*

Proverbs 6:9-11

The reality is that we need other people in our life in order to help us be resilient in times of crisis. If we live life for ourselves instead of living the life of loving others as God instructs us, we will find ourselves alone when we most need help.

> *Two are better than one, because they have a good return for their work: If one falls down, his friend can help him up. But pity the man who falls and has no one to help him up!*

Ecclesiastes 4:9-10

One of the key resources for resiliency is the people we have close relationships with. Friends that will be there in the tough times and help to pick us up when we need it are of immense value.

We began this chapter with some questions about the type of friend, employee, spouse, or parent you would like to have. Our final question is a restatement of these important questions.

Are you becoming the kind of person you would look for in a friend, employee, spouse, or parent?

Questions for Thought and Discussion

1. What character traits are most important to you in a friend? Why?

2. Which of the five relationship characteristics, discussed in this chapter, was most convicting to you? Why?

3. Have you found yourself drawn to people with any of the negative characteristics in your past relationships? Why?

4. What are some personal changes you need to make to become the type of person that benefits a relationship?

5. How have your beliefs about relationships impacted your ability to be resilient in the past?

Beliefs about Temptation

All of us have experienced those times when despite our intention to do the right thing, we give in to the temptation to do the wrong thing. Temptation is a reality of life. Understanding temptation and knowing how to resist the temptation to make the wrong choice will make us more resilient. Not falling into the hole is much preferred to having to repeatedly climb out of the hole.

First, we must understand what temptation is. Temptation is the enticement to do evil. It is not, in itself, sin. Jesus was tempted, yet the Bible says He was without sin. It is when we continue to entertain the temptation and are drawn into the evil that we have failed.

I would like to begin with two examples of temptation from the Bible that will help us to understand how temptation works and how we can be successful in the face of temptation.

The Temptation of Adam and Eve

The first is in the opening chapters of Genesis, the first book of the Bible. It is the temptation of Adam and Eve. We are told that

Satan came to Eve in the form of a serpent or snake, and began by questioning Eve about God's instructions to them.

Now the serpent was more crafty than any of the wild animals the LORD God had made. He said to the woman, "Did God really say, 'You must not eat from any tree in the garden'?

Genesis 3:1

God had given Adam and Eve freedom in the Garden of Eden to eat from any fruit in the Garden except that of one tree. They had the choice to love and obey God or to disobey Him and rebel against His authority in their life. Eve answered the serpent in the next verses:

The woman said to the serpent, "We may eat fruit from the trees in the garden, but God did say, 'You must not eat fruit from the tree that is in the middle of the garden, and you must not touch it, or you will die.'"

Genesis 3:2-3

Eve accurately reports what God has said with the exception of adding an instruction not to touch it. In the serpent's response, he begins to offer the temptation to Eve to disobey God:

You will not certainly die," the serpent said to the woman. "For God knows that when you eat from it your eyes will be opened, and you will be like God, knowing good and evil."

Genesis 3:4-5

In this response, Satan accomplishes two things. First, he directly contradicts God's instructions, "You will not surely die!" In doing so, he implies that God has not been truthful. Second, he indirectly questions God's motives in giving Adam and Eve the command with the statement, "God knows..." Up until this point, Eve had no reason to even question God's instruction. He had provided them with a perfect environment with everything they would ever want or need. Satan's statement raised the questions in Eve's mind, "Is there more? Is there something we are missing?" As she begins to question God's motives, it is now conceivable for her to disobey God. Eve next considers all of the reasons she might want to eat of this forbidden fruit:

When the woman saw that the fruit of the tree was good for food and pleasing to the eye, and also desirable for gaining wisdom, she took some and ate it. She also gave some to her husband, who was with her, and he ate it.

Genesis 3:6

Eve gives in to the temptation, and as is often the case, she draws others into her sin, her husband, Adam. Their sin would have consequences for all of humanity.

Three important principles come to mind as we consider this event:

1. Sin is ultimately a rebellion against God and His authority in our lives. We may also sin against other people but sin always is an offense to God.

2. Temptation is always ineffective when we are in right relationship with God. We must first be drawn away from God before we will consider disobeying Him.

3. Sin always has dire consequences. In this case, sin and death were introduced to all mankind and Adam and Eve were driven from the Garden of Eden to toil in a world that was now full of evil.

While our first example of temptation ended tragically, our second example gives us hope and strength for victory over temptation.

The Temptation of Jesus

The temptation of Jesus is reported in Matthew 4:1-11 and begins with Jesus being led into the desert by the Spirit of God for 40 days of fasting. Jesus had to be suffering from extreme hunger, and this is where Satan begins his temptation. He challenges Jesus to turn stones into bread. Jesus knew, however, that His fasting was not about food, but was about being totally focused on listening to God. Jesus quotes from the Old Testament scriptures:

> *Man shall not live on bread alone, but on every word that comes from the mouth of God.'"*

Matthew 4:4

Satan next tempts Jesus to prove Himself by jumping from the pinnacle of the temple. How often temptation comes to us with the words "I dare you..." Satan even quotes Scripture to show that God has promised to protect Him. Jesus, recognizing the real reason behind the challenge responds:

> *It is also written: 'Do not put the Lord your God to the test.'"*

Matthew 4:7

Finally, Satan goes all in by offering to give Jesus the whole world, if Jesus would only worship him. Jesus sees clearly the sin in Satan's bargain and responds:

> *"Away from me, Satan! For it is written: 'Worship the Lord your God, and serve him only.'"*

Matthew 4:10

Why was Jesus so successful in repelling the attacks of Satan? I believe there are two lessons we can learn from this temptation that will protect us in our moment of temptation.

1. Jesus was in unity and full fellowship with God. While He may have been weak physically, He was strong spiritually.

131

2. Jesus knew and depended on the truth of God's Word and refused to entertain anything contrary to its teaching.

The Pattern of Temptation

It would be helpful in our battle with temptation to have a better understanding of how temptation gets us to do things that are clearly harmful and not in our best interests. Fortunately, God outlines the pattern of nearly all temptation in James 1:13-17

> *When tempted, no one should say, "God is tempting me." For God cannot be tempted by evil, nor does he tempt anyone; but each person is tempted when they are dragged away by their own evil desire and enticed. Then, after desire has conceived, it gives birth to sin; and sin, when it is full-grown, gives birth to death.*

James 1:13-15

The first step as we have seen in the temptations above is that we are drawn away from God, and we become vulnerable to the tempter's claims. As long as we walk close to God and are listening only to His voice, we cannot be enticed by evil.

This is, however, a problem for us because ever since Adam and Eve sinned, every human being has been born with a sin nature which is predisposed to choose evil over good. This is in effect our "default mode." Unless we consciously choose otherwise, we are doomed to make the wrong decision every time. Paul describes it this way:

> *So I say, walk by the Spirit, and you will not gratify the desires of the flesh. For the flesh desires what is contrary to the Spirit, and the Spirit what is contrary to the flesh. They are in conflict with each other, so that you are not to do whatever you want.*

Galatians 5:16-17

It is only when we are close to God that we have the spiritual strength to withstand temptation. As James says:

Submit yourselves, then, to God. Resist the devil, and he will flee from you. Come near to God and he will come near to you.

James 4:7-8

The second step in this process is when we are presented with the enticement to sin. In this moment, it is important for us to recognize both the source of the temptation and the nature of all temptations. The ultimate source of all temptation is Satan, who the Bible describes as one who seeks to devour and destroy us.

Be alert and of sober mind. Your enemy the devil prowls around like a roaring lion looking for someone to devour.

1 Peter 5:8

In his attack on us, Satan employs three basic attacks outlined in 1 John:

Do not love the world or anything in the world. If anyone loves the world, love for the Father is not in them. For everything in the world—the lust of the flesh, the lust of the eyes, and the pride of life—comes not from the Father but from the world.

1 John 2:15-16

1. He appeals to our natural cravings and desires. God has given us many desires and has provided the means by which we can satisfy those desires whether they be hunger, sexual desires, material desires or any number of other desires. It is when we seek to satisfy those desires in sinful ways that we fail.

2. He appeals to the lust of the eyes. How many temptations begin with a glance and as we linger we are drawn into the temptation like the proverbial moth to the flame.

3. His last appeal is to our pride. In our pride, we want to do things in our own way; we refuse to admit that we are wrong in the face of obvious and overwhelming evidence and we reject God's authority in our life.

As I stated earlier, it is also important to recognize the nature of all temptation. Temptations have two basic features we need to be aware of:

1. The appeal of the temptation is a lie. It is a counterfeit of the real thing and will never satisfy like the real thing. Satan is the father of lies and the enemy of truth. While his offers may sound and look good, it is only an illusion. If we buy what he is selling, we will always be disappointed.

2. What pleasure there may be in pursuing sin is always temporary and is always followed by the consequences. Satan's temptations eventually lead to regrets, hurts, and brokenness

If we keep these two things in mind when we are faced with an enticing situation, we will be better able to see through temptation's claims and see the destruction they bring before we become its victim.

The third step in the pattern of temptation is the choice we make. In every temptation, we have two basic choices. We can give in to the temptation, or we can choose to obey God instead. While this may sound simple, it is often a struggle. Years ago, I memorized a Bible verse that has helped me repeatedly in facing temptation.

No temptation has overtaken you except what is common to mankind. And God is faithful; he will not let you be tempted beyond what you can bear. But when you are tempted, he will also provide a way out so that you can endure it.

1 Corinthians 10:13

This verse outlines a strategy for making the right choice in every situation:

1. Our temptation is not unique or insurmountable. If Satan can get us to believe that our situation is unique, then we can justify our disobedience since no one could be expected to resist such a temptation.

2. God will only allow you to face temptations you are able to resist with His help. We are not alone in temptation. The reason we need to stay near to God is to draw on His strength and His protection from temptations that might overwhelm us.

3. There is always a way to escape the temptation. It may not be easy, and it may cost us something to make the right decision, but there is always a way out. Our problem is that usually we choose the first thing that comes to mind (remember the "default mode" of our sin nature) and we rarely look very hard for the way of escape.

Once we have made our choice, we move onto the consequences of our decision. There are two types of consequences of making the wrong decision. The first is the natural consequences of the sin itself. These could include such things as:

- The legal consequences of an unlawful act

- The lack of trust that results from our lies and deception

- The broken relationship, unwanted pregnancy or STD that results from sexual immorality

- The destruction of our health and hurt to others resulting from gluttony, alcoholism or drug use

These are all the natural consequences of sinful choices, but they are not the only consequences we will suffer. We will also suffer from our separation from God as Isaiah the prophet describes:

> *But your iniquities have separated you from your God; your sins have hidden his face from you, so that he will not hear.*

Isaiah 59:2

Not only does making the sinful choice carry consequences but making the right choice also has its consequences.

> *Don't be deceived, my dear brothers and sisters. Every good and perfect gift is from above, coming down from the Father of the heavenly lights, who does not change like shifting shadows.*

James 1:16-17

This verse reminds us that God is the source of "every good and perfect gift." Why is this important? It is important because the world would have us to believe that to some degree we must disobey God's restrictive commands in order to really enjoy life. The reality is that disobeying God always leads to damaging consequences and guilt while obedience to God results in the enjoyment of those "good and perfect gifts."

Temptation can never be viewed as something trivial if we are to be resilient in life. When we find ourselves in a crisis, whether by our own fault or not, the answer is never another bad decision.

Questions for Thought and Discussion

1. What are some things we can learn from the failure of Adam and Eve in the face of temptation?

2. What are some things we can learn from the success of Jesus in the face of temptation?

3. How does accepting God as the source of "every good and perfect gift" impact the way we respond to temptation?

4. What do you need to do to make yourself more successful in resisting temptation?

5. How have your beliefs about temptation impacted your ability to be resilient in the past?

Beliefs about Change

When we find ourselves in a crisis and have determined that our defective beliefs have at least contributed to the problem, if not being the cause of the crisis, it is imperative that we accept that change is required.

Personal change is always necessary for us to respond differently than we have in the past and demonstrate resilience in our personal lives. Also, the nature of the change we must make (changing our beliefs and not just our decisions) is the most difficult kind of change, challenging deeply held beliefs that we must admit have been faulty.

Why is Change so Difficult?

Change is difficult for a variety of reasons. I would suggest that one major reason change is difficult, is simply inertia. Inertia is defined as the tendency of an object in motion to stay in motion and an object at rest to stay at rest and a sort of inertia often keeps us from being open to change. It is just easier to do what we have always done than to go through the effort to change. It is also much more difficult to start something new or change habits than it is to do nothing different.

I've been told that an airplane uses more energy to take off and reach cruising altitude, than it does to fly for the remainder of most journeys. There is just so much to overcome on take-off. The force of long-established habits is also difficult to overcome when we are contemplating change.

Fear is also a great detriment to attempting change in our lives. This fear can take many forms. The greatest fear is often the fear of failure. We are reluctant to attempt change because we are afraid that we won't be successful. In our fear, we often choose not to attempt the change.

We can also be fearful of unknown outcomes when we attempt a change in our lives. How will this change affect my life? What will be the responses of the important people in my life? Will I be able to sustain the change? Will this change really bring the benefits I am expecting? All of these questions can lead to emotional paralysis that keeps us from attempting transformational change in our lives

Past negative experiences with change can also make us reluctant to attempt change. Changes that were poorly planned or change that was made simply for the sake of change and not because it was needed, will leave us with a bad experience.

Essentials for Change

Motivation

This may be the most important essential for change. Many a person has begun to make a change in their life with good intentions, only to later lose the desire and motivation needed to follow through with the needed change. Motivation addresses the question "Why do I want to change?" The answer to this question is important because change can often be difficult and knowing clearly the reason for the change can help us to persevere in making the transformation. The answer to our motivation can include any of the following:

- **Personal Conscience** – God has given us an inner voice that directs us to make good choices and change things that are not consistent with God's desire for our lives. The Bible describes our conscience this way:

  Whether you turn to the right or to the left, your ears will hear a voice behind you, saying, "This is the way; walk in it."

  Isaiah 30:21

  This inner voice can be a strong motivator, providing a moral and spiritual imperative to the change we want to make.

- **Information** – When we learn a better way of doing something, we are prompted to implement the change in our lives. Life experience, education or even trial and error can lead us to the realization that the way we have been doing things isn't really the best approach. In this situation, it becomes necessary to adapt by changing the way we do things.

  Scripture contains many instructions for living life that may run counter to the culture we live in and the way we have learned to do things. As we choose to do things God's way, we will of necessity, make changes based on this information. Consider the claims made in the opening verses of the book of Proverbs, about the greatest source of wisdom:

  The proverbs of Solomon son of David, king of Israel: for attaining wisdom and discipline; for understanding words of insight; for acquiring a disciplined and prudent life, doing what is right and just and fair; for giving prudence to the simple,

140

knowledge and discretion to the young— let the wise listen and add to their learning, and let the discerning get guidance.

Proverbs 1:1-5

- **Unacceptable consequences or potential rewards** – Sometimes our experiences, either positive or negative, can be the motivation for life change. While trying something that works for us can encourage us to do it again, a negative outcome can also be a strong motivator to not repeat the mistake again. In the Old Testament, God told His people that obedience to Him would result in blessings and disobedience would lead to curses, leaving the individual with a clear choice, not only of compliance with God but also as to the outcomes resulting from those decisions.

This day I call the heavens and the earth as witnesses against you that I have set before you life and death, blessings and curses. Now choose life, so that you and your children may live

Deuteronomy 30:19

- **Spiritual Transformation** – When God begins to work in our lives, God changes us! Someone has said, "God loves you just the way you are, but God loves you too much to leave you just the way you are." As we grow in our relationship with God, change is imperative. It is also something that God initiates as He works His creative power in our lives, giving us new life in Him.

Therefore, if anyone is in Christ, he is a new creation; the old has gone, the new has come!

2 Corinthians 5:17

These motivations, among others, will often determine the success or failure of our attempts at change. Without a strong and clear motivation, we will be tempted to give up when the process of change becomes difficult.

Transformed Thinking

The second key to positive change is transformed thinking. The reason we need to change is because some aspect of our life is not what we want it to be. This is, as we have seen, because one or more of our beliefs is inconsistent with truth and reality. We know that before our outcomes can change, our decisions must change and those will only change when we transform our beliefs. This transformation of our beliefs happens as we bring them into alignment with God's Word and the truth we learn it its pages. Paul challenges his readers to transform their thinking by the renewing of their mind:

> *Do not conform to the pattern of this world, but be transformed by the renewing of your mind. Then you will be able to test and approve what God's will is—his good, pleasing and perfect will.*

Romans 12:2

This transformed thinking is always consistent with God's will for our life, which is in turn, good, pleasing and perfect. Note that the opposite of transformed thinking is thinking that fits the pattern of the world around us. If we are to be agents of change, there is no room for conformity to the status quo.

Empowerment

Knowledge and desire for change are of little value if we feel powerless to affect the desired change. It is very easy to be discouraged by past attempts at change and assume we are powerless even when we may indeed have the power to change. The Christian is assured of God's power in our lives even when we feel powerless.

But he said to me, "My grace is sufficient for you, for my power is made perfect in weakness." Therefore I will boast all the more gladly about my weaknesses, so that Christ's power may rest on me. That is why, for Christ's sake, I delight in weaknesses, in insults, in hardships, in persecutions, in difficulties. For when I am weak, then I am strong.

2 Corinthians 12:9-10

Now to him who is able to do immeasurably more than all we ask or imagine, according to his power that is at work within us.

Ephesians 3:20

God has the power to enact change in our life and when we feel weak and powerless, He is then able to demonstrate that power, demonstrating that what has been done could only have been accomplished through God's power at work in us.

Action

Any plan for change is useless until it is put in action. Change requires that we DO things differently. It is only when we take action that we see the results of change. Many people have good intentions for change but without action, those intentions are worthless. No one ever lost weight by simply intending to exercise. It is when we follow through on our intentions with action that change happens.

Dear children, let us not love with words or tongue but with actions and in truth.

1 John 3:18

Encouragement and Endurance

Some changes are difficult and may require repeated efforts, and in these situations, it is essential that we build into our plan a system for our support when the process gets discouraging. As Christians, we are instructed to engage in the encouragement and strengthening of each other. This makes the church uniquely equipped to be places where positive change is a way of life.

> *Therefore encourage one another and build each other up, just as in fact you are doing.*

1 Thessalonians 5:11

Not only are we to receive encouragement from each other, but we also can be encouraged by our study of the Scriptures. The historical accounts and instructions in Scripture give us the tools we need to effect change in our lives and receive encouragement and strength for the difficult process.

> *For everything that was written in the past was written to teach us, so that through the endurance taught in the Scriptures and the encouragement they provide we might have hope.*

Romans 15:4

Change is at the same time inevitable and exciting, transforming and scary. Our attitude toward change will significantly affect our ability to be resilient in a time of crisis. It is my hope and prayer that this book will encourage you to overcome whatever crisis you are facing and be resilient. Through resilience, our future does not have to be the same as our past. We have the power to bounce back stronger than ever.

Questions for Thought and Discussion

1. What is at least one change you would like to begin making in your life in the next 30 days?

2. What is your motivation for making this change? How could your motivation be strengthened?

3. What are the biggest barriers to your implementing changes in your life?

4. How do you tend to respond to change in your life? What do you need to do to be more accepting of positive changes?

5. How have your beliefs about change impacted your ability to be resilient in the past?

Made in the USA
Columbia, SC
19 January 2018